M000073367

Back to Basics: Cryptocurrency Investing

by Kiana Danial

WILEY

Publisher's Acknowledgments

Author: Kiana Danial

Senior Acquisitions Editor:
Tracy Boggier

Project Manager:
Michelle Hacker

Compilation Editor:
Georgette Beatty

Production Editor:
Mohammed Zafar Ali

Cover Photo: (stairs)
© FrankRamspott / Getty Images,
(litecoin) © logoff / Getty Images,
(bitcoin) © FrankRamspott /
Getty Images

Back to Basics:
Cryptocurrency Investing

Published by John Wiley & Sons, Inc.
111 River St.
Hoboken, NJ 07030-5774
http://www.wiley.com

For general information on our other products and services, please contact our Business Development
Department in the U.S. at 317-572-3205.

ISBN 978-1-119-55133-1 (pbk)

Manufactured in the United States of America

F10006499_112818

Table of Contents

1

Cryptocurrencies as an Investment

Whether you're a seasoned investor who has been exposed only to investment assets other than cryptos or you're starting to invest for the first time, you're probably wondering why you should consider including cryptocurrencies in your portfolio. What's the big deal about all these coins anyway?

In this chapter, you get an overview of cryptocurrencies. That way, you can decide whether the cryptocurrency industry is the right route for you to grow your wealth.

Cryptocurrencies versus Traditional Investments

Diversification is the good old "don't put all your eggs in one basket" thing. You can apply this advice to literally anything in life. If you're grocery shopping, don't buy only apples. Even though they say "an apple a day keeps the doctor away," you still need the nutrition in other kinds of vegetables and fruit.

You can go about investment diversification in so many ways. You can diversify with different financial assets, like stocks, bonds, foreign exchange (forex), and so on. You can diversify based on industry, like technology, healthcare, and entertainment. You can allocate your investment by having multiple investment time frames, both short-term and long-term. Adding cryptocurrencies to your investment portfolio is essentially one way of balancing that portfolio. Especially because the cryptocurrency industry is vastly different from traditional ones, this diversification may increase the potential of maximizing your portfolio's growth. One of the main reasons for this higher potential is that the cryptocurrency market may react differently to various global and financial events.

The following sections briefly look into some of the traditional markets and explore their differences from the cryptocurrency market.

Stocks

The stock market gives you the opportunity to take a bite of the profits a company makes. By buying stocks of that company, you become a part-owner of that firm. The more stocks you buy, the bigger your slice of the cake. And of course, the higher the risk you face if the whole cake is thrown out in the garbage.

The stock market is perhaps one of the most appealing investment assets. Novice investors may pick up a stock or two just because they like the company. For most investors, the charm of stock investing is the possibility that the prices will increase over time and generate significant capital gains. Some stocks even provide you with a periodic income stream through something called *dividends.* (Find out more about capital gains and dividend income later in this chapter.) Regardless, for most stocks, the dividends paid within a year are nothing compared to the increase of the stock's value, especially when the economic environment is upbeat.

This is precisely what stocks and cryptocurrencies have in common: When their respective markets are strong, you can generally expect to benefit from price appreciation.

Make no mistake, though, both markets have their bad days and sometimes even bad years. The stock market has a longer history that can guide investors through navigating the future. For example, even though it may not always seem like it, bad days happen less often than good ones. For the 70 years between 1947 and 2017, the Dow, one of the main stock market indexes, ended the year at a lower price only 28.6 percent of the time (20 years). The other 71.4 percent (50 years), it went up.

However, stock investing naturally has some disadvantages:

- **Stocks face different types of risks.** Even the most awesome stocks have risks that you can't easily eliminate, such as the following: business and financial risk, purchasing power risk, market risk, event risk, government control and regulations, foreign competition, and the general state of the economy.

- **The stock selection process can be a pain in the neck.** You have literally thousands of stocks to choose from. Predicting how the company will perform tomorrow also can be very difficult. After all, the price today only reflects the current state of the company or what the market participants perceive it to be.

By investing in the cryptocurrency market, you may be able to balance out some of the preceding risks. The cryptocurrency selection process is also different from that of stocks, as I explain in Chapter 3.

The final disadvantage of stock investing, however, is similar to that of crypto investing. They both generally produce less current income than some other investments. Several types of investments, such as bonds (see the following section), pay more current income and do so with much greater certainty.

Bonds

Bonds are also known as *fixed-income securities*. They're different from cryptocurrencies and stocks in that you loan money to an entity for a period of time, and you receive a fixed amount of interest on a periodic basis — hence its categorization as "fixed income."

Just like with cryptocurrencies and stocks (see the preceding section), you can also expect capital gains from bonds. But these capital gains work a bit differently. Because the company issuing bonds promises to repay a fixed amount when the bonds mature, bond prices don't typically rise in correlation with the firm's profits. The bond prices rise and fall as market interest rates change.

Another similarity among bonds, cryptocurrencies, and stocks is that they're all issued by a wide range of companies. Additionally, many governmental bodies issue bonds. So if you're looking to diversify only within the bonds market, you still can choose from a range of relatively safe ones to highly speculative ones.

Compared to cryptocurrencies and stocks, bonds are generally less risky and provide higher current income. But they still are subject to a variety of risks. Some of the risks involved with bonds investing are similar to those of cryptocurrencies and stocks — namely, purchasing power risk, business and financial risk, and liquidity risk. Bonds have an additional type of risk known as the *call risk* or *prepayment risk.* Call risk is the risk that a bond will be *called,* or retired, long before its maturity date. If the bond issuer calls its bonds, you'll have to find another place for your funds.

The potential for very high returns on bonds is much lower compared to cryptocurrencies and stocks. But the risk involved with bonds is also comparatively lower. You can find more about cryptocurrency risks later in this chapter.

Forex

Here's an alternative investment that may be even riskier than cryptocurrencies. *Forex* is the geek term for the foreign exchange market. By participating in the forex market, you buy and sell currencies — not cryptocurrencies, but fiat currencies such as the U.S. dollar, the euro, the British pound, the Australian dollar, or any other currency any government issues. A *fiat currency* is a country's legal tender that's issued by the government.

Before Bitcoin became the celebrity of financial assets in 2017, most people associated cryptocurrencies such as Bitcoin with the traditional forex market because "cryptocurrency" includes the word "currency," and crypto owners hoped to use their assets to make payments. However, as mentioned earlier in this chapter, cryptocurrencies also have a lot in common with stocks.

When you participate in the forex market, you don't necessarily invest for long-term capital gains. Even the most popular currencies such as the U.S. dollar are subject to a ton of volatility throughout the year. A good U.S. economy doesn't always translate into a stronger U.S. dollar.

Participating in the forex market as an investor mainly consists of short-to-medium-term trading activity between different currency pairs. You can buy the euro versus the U.S. dollar (the EUR/USD pair), for example. If the euro's value appreciates relative to the U.S. dollar's, you make money. However, if the U.S. dollar's value goes higher than the euro's, you lose money.

Analyzing the forex market needs a very different approach when compared to stock and cryptocurrency analysis. When looking at the forex markets, you need to focus on the issuing country's economic state, its upcoming economic figures such as its gross domestic product (GDP, or the value of the goods produced inside the country), unemployment rate, inflation, interest rate, and so on, as well as its political environment.

However, just like the cryptocurrency market, you need to trade forex in pairs. You can compare these pairs to dancing couples — international couples who push each other back and forth. Traders can make money by speculating which direction the couple will move next.

You can apply a similar concept to the cryptocurrency market. For example, you can pair up Bitcoin (BTC) and

Ethereum (ETH) against each other. You can even pair up a cryptocurrency such as Bitcoin against a fiat currency such as the U.S. dollar and speculate their value against each other. However, in these cases you need to analyze each currency, crypto or fiat, separately. Then you need to measure their relative value against each other and predict which currency will win the couple's battle in the future.

You can also consider cryptocurrencies as a cross between stocks and forex. Though many investors invest in cryptocurrencies for capital gain purposes, you can also trade different cryptocurrencies against each other, the way you can in the forex market (see Chapter 3).

Precious metals

It's time to compare one of the most recent manmade means to buy stuff (cryptocurrencies) to one of the most ancient ones. Before the advent of paper money, precious metals such as gold and silver were long used to make coins and to buy stuff.

Back in the days of bartering, people would exchange stuff that provided real value to their human needs: chickens, clothes, or farming services. Supposedly, people in the ancient civilization of Lydia were among the first to use coins made of gold and silver in exchange for goods and services. This change was followed by leather money, paper money, credit cards, and now cryptocurrencies.

Precious metals have long been a favorite investment tool among market participants. One of the main reasons is their historical association with wealth. Often, when investments such as bonds, real estate, and the stock market go down or the political environment is uncertain, people flock to precious metals. People prefer to own precious metals at these times because they can actually physically touch metals and keep them in their homes right next to their beds.

Besides the fact that you need to mine in order to get your hands on precious metals and some cryptocurrencies, one key similarity between precious metals and cryptocurrencies is that both categories have unregulated characteristics. Gold has been an unregulated currency at various times and in various places. Unregulated currencies become more valuable when investors don't trust the official currency, and cryptocurrencies just seem to be another example of this trend. (I talk about cryptocurrency mining in Chapter 4.)

Investing in precious metals comes with a number of risk factors you need to keep in mind. For example, if you're buying physical precious metals as an investment, you must consider their portability risk. Transferring precious metals can be expensive given their weight, high import taxes, and the need for a high level of security. In contrast, you don't need to make a physical transfer with cryptocurrencies, besides the hardware crypto wallets I discuss in Chapter 3. But moving cryptocurrencies is much faster and less expensive, even with a hardware wallet, than transferring precious metals.

On the other hand, cryptocurrency prices have been more volatile in the short time they've been available on the markets than all precious metals combined have. The 2017 volatility in particular was due to hype in the market. As cryptocurrency investing becomes more mainstream and more people use it for everyday transactions, crypto prices may become more predictable.

Cryptocurrency Returns

Different assets generate different types of returns. For example, one source of return is the change in the investment's value. Also, when you invest in the stock market or the forex (foreign exchange) market, you may generate income in the form of dividends or interest. Investors call these two sources of return *capital gains* (or *capital losses*) and *current income*, respectively. Although most people invest in the cryptocurrency market for capital gains, some cryptocurrencies actually offer current income opportunities.

Capital gains (or losses)

The most popular reason for crypto investing is to see gains in the coins' value. Some people associate the coins with precious metals such as gold. Doing so makes sense because, just like gold, a limited amount is available for most cryptocurrencies, and one way to extract many of them is to mine. (Head to Chapter 4 for details on cryptocurrency mining.)

With that, many investors consider cryptocurrencies to be assets even though they're technically currencies that can be used in transactions. People buy these currencies in hopes of selling them when the prices rise more. If the value of your cryptocurrency token goes higher from the time you purchase, you get capital gains when you sell the token. Congrats! If the prices go lower, you end up with capital losses.

_____

_____

_____

Income

Income is a lesser-known type of return in the cryptocurrency market. Income is generated from something called *crypto dividends.*

Traditionally, dividends occur when public companies distribute a portion of their earnings to their shareholders. Traditional types of dividends include cash payments, shares of stock, or other property.

Earning dividends in the crypto market can get a bit more complicated. Different currencies have different operating systems and their own rules and regulations. However, the concept still remains the same. Crypto dividend payments are becoming increasingly popular among altcoins, which are the alternative cryptocurrencies besides Bitcoin. When choosing a cryptocurrency for your portfolio, you can consider looking into crypto dividends as well as the potential of capital gains (discussed in the preceding section).

Some of the most popular ways to earn crypto dividends are staking (holding a proof-of-stake coin in a special wallet) and holding (buying and holding a crypto in any wallet).

At the time of writing, some dividend-paying crypto-currencies include NEO, KuCoin, BridgeCoin, Neblio, and Komodo (see Chapter 2). In addition, besides staking and holding, you can earn regular interest payments by participating in crypto lending. For example, you can earn up to 5 percent interest on your cryptos by allowing companies like Celsius Network to give out loans to the general public against cryptos.

Different Kinds of Risk

Investment returns are exciting, but you can't consider return without also looking at risk. The sad truth about any type of investment is that the greater the expected return, the greater the risk. Because cryptocurrencies are considered riskier than some other assets, they may also provide higher returns. The relationship between risk and return is called the *risk-return tradeoff*.

Cryptocurrency investing isn't a get-rich-quick scheme. You shouldn't invest in cryptocurrencies by using your life savings or taking out a loan. You must consider your risk tolerance, understand the different sources of cryptocurrency risks, and then develop an investment strategy that's suitable for you — just you, not anyone else — because you're unique, and so is your financial situation.

Also keep in mind that early Bitcoin investors waited years to see any returns. If you don't have the patience required to see meaningful returns on your investment, you may need to forget about investing altogether.

That being said, a healthy amount of risk appetite is essential not only when investing but also in life. Getting educated about risk puts you right on top of your game. Knowing your risk tolerance, you can create a strategy that protects you and your wealth. The risks associated with cryptocurrencies come from many different sources.

Crypto hype risk

The main reason cryptos have a lot of hype is that most people don't know about what they're investing in; they just end up listening to the crowd. The crypto hype back in 2017 was one of the many drivers of the fast-and-furious market surge. After people started to figure out what they'd invested in, the prices crashed.

Before falling for the market noise, arm yourself with knowledge on the specific cryptos you're considering. You have plenty of opportunities to make lots of money in the crypto market. Be patient and acquire the right knowledge instead of betting on the current hype. An investor who trades on the hype probably doesn't even have an investment strategy — unless you call gambling a strategy. You can find different methods of strategy development in Chapter 5.

Security risk

Scams. Hacking. Theft. These issues have been a common theme in the cryptocurrency market since Bitcoin's inception in 2009. And with each scandal, the cryptocurrencies' values are compromised as well, although temporarily. Your cryptocurrencies can be compromised in three main ways. You should definitely follow safety precautions in every step of your cryptocurrency investing strategy.

Safety check #1: The cryptocurrency itself

Hundreds of cryptocurrencies are already available for investments, with thousands of new ICOs (initial coin offerings) on the way (see Chapter 5). When choosing a cryptocurrency to invest in, you must educate yourself on the blockchain's protocol and make sure no bugs (or rumors of bugs) may compromise your investment. The *protocol* is the common set of rules that the blockchain network has agreed upon. You may be able to find out about the nature of the cryptocurrency's protocol on its white paper on its website. The *white paper* is an official document that the crypto founders put together before their ICO, laying out everything there is to know about the cryptocurrency. But companies are unlikely to share their shortcomings in their white papers. That's why reading reviews on savvy websites like Reddit and my site, InvestDiva.com, can often be your best bet.

These types of bugs appear even in major cryptocurrencies. For example, a lot of negative press surrounded EOS's release of the first version of its open-source software before June 2, 2018. A Chinese security firm had found a bug in the EOS code that could theoretically have been used to create tokens out of thin air. However, EOS was able to fix the bugs. To further turn the bad press into positive, Block.one, the developer of EOS, invited people to hunt for undiscovered bugs in return for monetary rewards (a process known as a *bug bounty*).

Reliable cryptocurrency issuers should take matters into their own hands immediately when a bug is found. But until they do, you're wise to keep your hands off their coins.

Safety check #2: The exchange

Exchanges are where you trade cryptocurrency tokens (see Chapter 3). You need to <u>make sure</u> that <u>your trading host</u> is <u>trustworthy and credible</u>. Countless numbers of security incidents and data breaches have occurred in the crypto community because of the exchanges; <u>centralized exchanges are the most vulnerable to attacks.</u> Many exchanges are keeping up with the latest safety measures. However, exchange hacks still happen almost on a monthly basis.

As time goes by, the market learns from previous mistakes and works on a better and safer future. However, you still need to take matters into your own hands as much as possible. Before choosing an exchange, take a <u>look at its security section</u> on its website. Check on whether it participates in any bug bounty programs to encourage safety. And ask the right people about the exchange.

Safety check #3: Your wallet

The final round of security check is all in your own hands because what kind of crypto wallet you use is entirely up to you. Though you don't physically carry your crypto coins, you can store them in a secure physical wallet. You actually store the public and private keys, which you can use for making transactions with your altcoins, in these wallets as well. You can take your wallet's security to a higher level by using a backup. I explore wallets more in Chapter 3.

Volatility risk

Volatility risk is essentially the risk in unexpected market movements. Though volatility can be a good thing, it can also catch you off guard sometimes. Just like any other market, the cryptocurrency market can suddenly move in the opposite direction from what you expected. If you aren't prepared for market volatility, you can lose the money you invested in the market.

The volatility in the cryptocurrency market has resulted from many factors. For one, it's a brand-new technology. The inception of revolutionary technologies — such as the Internet — can create initial periods of volatility. Blockchain technology (covered later in this chapter) and its underpinning cryptocurrencies take a lot of getting used to before they become mainstream.

The best way to combat the cryptocurrency volatility risk is looking at the big picture. Volatility matters a lot if you have a short-term investing horizon because it's an indicator of how much money you may make or lose over a short period.

But if you have a long-term horizon, volatility can turn into an opportunity.

Liquidity risk

By definition, *liquidity risk* is the risk of not being able to sell (or *liquidate*) an investment quickly at a reasonable price. Liquidity is important for any tradable asset. The forex market is considered the most liquid market in the world. But even in the forex market, the lack of liquidity may be a problem. If you trade currencies with very low volume, you may not even be able to close your trade because the prices just won't move.

Cryptocurrencies can also see episodes of illiquidity. The liquidity problem was one of the factors that led to the high volatility in Bitcoin and other altcoins in 2017. When the liquidity is low, the risk of price manipulation also comes into play. One big player can easily move the market to his or her favor by placing a massive order. The crypto community refers to these types of big players as *whales*. In the cryptocurrency market, whales often move small altcoins by using their huge capital.

On the bright side, as cryptocurrency investing becomes more available and acceptable, the market may become more liquid. The increase in the number of trusted crypto exchanges will provide opportunity for more people to trade. Crypto ATMs and payment cards are popping up, helping raise the awareness and acceptance of cryptocurrencies in everyday transactions.

Another key factor in cryptocurrency liquidity is the stance of countries on cryptocurrency regulations. If the authorities are able to define issues such as consumer protection and crypto taxes, more people will be comfortable using and trading cryptocurrencies, which will affect their liquidity.

When choosing a cryptocurrency to trade, you must consider its liquidity by analyzing its acceptance, popularity, and the number of exchanges it's been traded on. Lesser-known cryptocurrencies may have a lot of upside potential, but they may put you in trouble because of lack of liquidity. I explore different types of cryptocurrencies and their characteristics in Chapter 2.

Vanishing risk

Hundreds of different cryptocurrencies are currently out there. More and more cryptocurrencies are being introduced every day. In ten years' time, many of these altcoins may vanish while others flourish.

A familiar example of vanishing risk is the dot-com bubble. In the late 1990s, many people around the world dreamed up businesses that capitalized on the popularity of the Internet. Some, such as Amazon and eBay, succeeded in conquering the world. Many more crashed and burned. Following the path of history, many of the booming cryptocurrencies popping up left and right are destined to bust.

To minimize the vanishing risk, you need to analyze the fundamentals of the cryptocurrencies you choose to invest in. Do their goals make sense to you? Are they solving a problem that will continue in the years to come? Who are their partners? You can't vanish the vanishing risk entirely (pun intended), but you can eliminate your exposure to a sudden bust. Check out Chapter 3 for more on fundamental analysis.

Regulation risk

One of the initial attractions of cryptocurrencies was their lack of regulation. In the good old days, crypto enthusiasts didn't have to worry about governments chasing them down. All they had was a white paper and a promise. However, as the demand for cryptocurrencies grows, global regulators are scratching their heads on how to keep up — and to not lose their shirts to the new economic reality. To date, most digital currencies aren't backed by any central government, meaning each country has different standards.

You can divide the cryptocurrency regulation risk into the regulation event risk and regulation's nature itself:

- The *regulation event risk* doesn't necessarily mean that the cryptocurrency market is doing poorly. It just means the market participants reacted to an unexpected announcement. In 2018, every seemingly small regulation announcement drove the price of many major cryptocurrencies and created a ton of volatility.

- At the time of writing, there are no global cryptocurrency regulators, so existing regulations are all over the board. In some countries (such as Japan and the United States), for example, cryptocurrency exchanges are legal as long as they're registered with the financial authorities. Some countries, such as China, have been stricter on the cryptocurrencies but more lenient on the blockchain industry itself.

The future of cryptocurrency regulations seems to be bright at this writing, but it may impact the markets in the future.

_____

_____

_____

As the market grows stronger, though, these impacts may turn into isolated events.

Tax risk

When cryptocurrency investing first got popular, hardly anyone was paying taxes on the gains. A lot of underreporting was going on. However, as the market gets more regulated, the authorities may become stricter on taxation. As of 2018, the U.S. Internal Revenue Service views Bitcoin and other cryptocurrencies as property, despite the fact that they have the word *currencies* in them. Therefore, transactions using altcoins are subject to capital gains tax.

If you live in the United States or are a U.S. citizen, tax risk involves the chance that the authorities may make unfavorable changes in tax laws, such as limitation of deductions, increase in tax rates, and elimination of tax exemptions. In other countries, tax risk can get more complicated. For example, at the time of writing, the Philippines hasn't clearly established whether the Bureau of Internal Revenue will treat cryptocurrencies as equities, property, or capital gains tax.

Although virtually all investments are vulnerable to increases in tax rates, cryptocurrency taxation is a fuzzy area.

<u>Most regulators can't even agree on the basic concept of what</u> <u>a token represents</u>. And of course, different countries, different rules. Doing your due diligence on taxing before developing your investment strategy is crucial. Flip to Chapter 3 for more details on taxes in relation to cryptocurrencies.

Blockchain Technology Basics

Modern technologies allow people to communicate directly. You can use them to directly send emails, text messages, pictures, and videos to others without the use of a middleman. This way, you can maintain trust with others no matter where they are in the world.

Despite this advancement, people still have to trust a third party to complete a financial transaction. But blockchain technology is challenging this setup in a radical way. I explain the basics of blockchain technology in the following sections.

What is a blockchain, and how does it work?

Simply put, a *blockchain* is a special kind of database. According to cigionline.org, the term *blockchain* refers to the whole network of distributed ledger technologies. According to Oxford Dictionaries, a *ledger* is "a book or other collection of financial accounts of a particular type." It can be a computer file that records transactions. A ledger is actually the foundation of accounting and is as old as writing and money.

Now imagine a whole suite of incorruptible digital ledgers of economic transactions that can be programmed to record and track not only financial transactions but also virtually everything of value. The blockchain can track things like medical records, land titles, and even voting. It's a shared, distributed, and immutable ledger that records the history of transactions starting with transaction number one. It establishes trust, accountability, and transparency.

Blockchain stores information in batches called *blocks*. These blocks are linked together in a sequential way to form a continuous line. A chain of blocks. A blockchain. Each block is like a page of a ledger or a record book. Each block mainly has three elements:

- **Data:** The type of data depends on what the blockchain is being used for. In Bitcoin, for example, a block's data contains the details about the transaction including sender, receiver, number of coins, and so on.

- **Hash:** A *hash* in blockchain is something like a fingerprint or signature. It identifies a block and all its content, and it's always unique.

- **Hash of previous block:** This piece is precisely what makes a blockchain. Because each block carries the information of the previous block, the chain becomes very secure.

Here's an example of how a bunch of blocks come together in a blockchain. Say you have three blocks. Block 1 contains this stuff:

- Data: 10 Bitcoins from Fred to Jack
- Hash (simplified): 12A
- Previous hash (simplified): 000

Block 2 contains this stuff:

- Data: 5 Bitcoins from Jack to Mary
- Hash (simplified): 3B4
- Previous hash: 12A

_____

_____

_____

Block 3 contains this stuff:

- Data: 4 Bitcoins from Mary to Sally
- Hash (simplified): C74
- Previous hash: 3B4

As you can see in Figure 1-1, each block has its own hash and a hash of the previous block. So block 3 points to block 2, and block 2 points to block 1. (*Note:* The first block is a bit special because it can't point to a previous block. This block is the *genesis block.*)

The hashes and the data are unique to each block, but they can still be tampered with. The following section lays out some ways blockchains secure themselves.

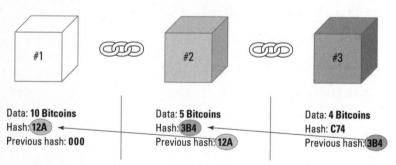

© John Wiley & Sons, Inc.

Figure 1-1: *Simplified version of how a blockchain works.*

How does a blockchain secure itself?

Interfering with a block on the blockchain is almost impossible to do. The first way a blockchain secures itself is by hashing. Tampering with a block within a blockchain causes the hash of the block to change. That change makes the following block, which originally pointed to the first block's hash, invalid. In fact, changing a single block makes all the following blocks invalid. This setup gives the blockchain a level of security.

However, using hashing isn't enough to prevent tampering. That's because computers these days are super fast, and they can calculate hundreds of thousands of hashes per second. Technically, a hacker can change the hash of a specific block and then calculate and change all the hashes of the following blocks in order to hide the tampering.

That's why on top of the hashes, blockchains have additional security steps including things like proof-of-work and peer-to-peer distribution. A *proof-of-work* (PoW) is a mechanism that slows down the creation of the blocks. In Bitcoin's case, for example, it takes about ten minutes to calculate the required PoW and add a new block to the chain. This timeline makes tampering with a block super difficult because if you interfere with one block, you need to interfere with all the following blocks. A blockchain like Bitcoin contains hundreds of thousands of blocks, so successfully manipulating it can take over ten years.

Another way blockchains secure themselves is by being distributed. Blockchains don't use a central entity to manage the chain. Instead, they use a *peer-to-peer* (P2P) network. In public blockchains like Bitcoin, everyone is allowed to join. Each member of the network is called a *validator* or a *node.* When someone joins the network, she gets the full copy of the blockchain. This way, the node can verify that everything is still in order.

Here's what happens when someone creates a new block in the network:

1. The new block is sent to everyone in the network.

2. Each node then verifies the block and makes sure it hasn't been tampered with.

3. If everything checks out, each node adds this new block to his or her own blockchain.

All the nodes in this process create a consensus. They agree about which blocks are valid and which ones aren't. The other nodes in the network reject blocks that are tampered with.

So to successfully mess with a block on a blockchain, you'd need to tamper with all the blocks on the chain, redo the proof-of-work for each block, and take control of the peer-to-peer network.

Blockchains are also constantly evolving. One of the most recent developments in the cryptocurrency ecosystem is the addition of something called a *smart contract*. A smart contract is a digital computer program stored inside a blockchain. It can directly control the transfer of cryptocurrencies or other digital assets based on certain conditions.

2

Types of Cryptocurrencies

By now, you probably have heard of the cryptocurrency that started it all: Bitcoin. But Bitcoin is hardly the only famous or even investment-worthy cryptocurrency out there anymore. So many other digital coins are available that have made massive improvements to the Bitcoin model to avoid its disadvantages.

In this chapter, I go over some of the most famous cryptos as of 2018. But because the cryptocurrency market is ever-changing, I explain how you can navigate your way through all the up-and-coming cryptos for years to come.

Celebrity Cryptocurrencies by Market Cap

One of the fastest ways to navigate through popular cryptocurrencies is to check out their ranking based on their *market capitalization*, or *market cap*. Traditionally, market cap is the value of a company that's traded on the stock market. You can calculate it by multiplying the total number of shares by the present share price.

In the cryptoworld, market capitalization shows the value of all units of a specific cryptocurrency that are for sale right now. To calculate a cryptocurrency's market cap, simply multiply the cryptocurrency's current price by its *circulating supply*. Circulating supply is the best approximate number of coins that are circulating in the market and in the general public's hands.

Knowing about a crypto's market cap and its ranking versus other coins is important because that info can quickly show you how popular the coin is and how much money you may be able to make from it. You can find out about all crypto-currencies' market caps by visiting websites such as http://coinmarketcap.com, www.cryptocompare.com/, https://coincodex.com/, and www.coingecko.com/.

Market cap can't tell you everything about a cryptocur-rency's investment potential. Lots of other factors, such as regulation, rumor, and so on, can affect a cryptocurrency's value. I talk more about analyzing a cryptocurrency's perfor-mance in Chapter 3.

 A higher market cap isn't necessarily a good thing. Investors who can take higher risks may prefer cryp-tocurrencies with a lower market cap because those may offer more room for the market cap to increase. However, if you want to play it safe and avoid vola-tility or vanishing risk (see Chapter 1), you may pre-fer going with cryptocurrencies with a higher market cap.

With a knowledge of what role a coin's market cap plays in the industry, you can start to evaluate cryptocurrencies based on that metric. I discuss Bitcoin and other major cryptocurrencies in the following sections.

Bitcoin

Ranking number one on the list, Bitcoin was developed in 2009. As of October 2018, Bitcoin's market cap is around $115 billion.

A bit of Bitcoin background

An entity called Satoshi Nakamoto invented Bitcoin. Satoshi claimed to be a man living in Japan, born on April 5, 1975. Most speculation about the true identity of Satoshi points to a number of cryptography and computer science experts of non-Japanese descent living in the United States and various European countries.

But Satoshi's anonymity isn't really a big deal because Bitcoin (and other cryptocurrencies, for that matter) are supposed to be open source and decentralized. In fact, according to Bitcoin.org, no single person or entity "owns the Bitcoin network much like no one owns the technology behind email." Bitcoin users around the world control Bitcoin, with the developer improving the software and forkers making some radical changes. However, the main idea behind Bitcoin and Bitcoin's protocol can't be changed.

Almost ten years after Satoshi published Bitcoin's white paper, Bitcoin's market cap went up to as much as $320 billion by the end of 2017. If you had invested $100 to buy one Bitcoin in 2011, you would've had $20,000 worth of Bitcoin by the end of 2017. Of course, many initial investors bought more than one Bitcoin at the time, which is exactly how all those Bitcoin millionaires were made. If you had bought 100 Bitcoins in 2011, by the end of 2017 they would have been worth $2 million.

But by the time everyone started talking about Bitcoin, it went crashing down to around $120 billion and stayed there for most of 2018. It maintained its number one ranking among all other cryptocurrencies, though. The main reason behind this position may be that most people have heard a lot (relatively speaking) about Bitcoin but not so much about other cryptocurrencies. So even though they have several hundred other altcoins to choose from, even some that may be better long-term alternatives to Bitcoin, most newbies who want to get involved in the market start out with Bitcoin.

Another reason for Bitcoin's huge market cap is its accessibility. I can pretty safely say that all cryptocurrency exchanges (see Chapter 3) carry Bitcoin. But not all exchanges list all altcoins, at least for now.

Bitcoin characteristics

Here are some main features of Bitcoin:

- Bitcoin's trading symbol is BTC.
- Bitcoin is minable.
- Coin creation occurs through proof-of-work (PoW).
- Transaction time is between 30 minutes and 24 hours.
- Transactions aren't fully anonymous.
- Bitcoin is decentralized.
- Mining Bitcoin requires a lot of (wasted) energy.

Generally speaking, the whole market sentiment follows the volatility of Bitcoin in longer-term time frames (with many past exceptions). You can use this piece of information in technical analysis for investing. You can find out more about Bitcoin on its website, https://bitcoin.org/.

Ethereum

Ranked number two based on coin market cap as of 2018, Ethereum is another major cryptocurrency. As of October 2018, its market cap is around $23 billion.

Brief Ethereum background

Compared to Bitcoin, Ethereum is a pretty young currency; Russian American Vitalik Buterin proposed it in 2013.

Ethereum uses the old Bitcoin's wisdom and philosophy, but it has a different purpose and capability. According to its website, `www.ethereum.org`, "Ethereum is a decentralized platform that runs smart contracts." *Smart contracts* allow people to create agreements without a middleman. Ethereum creates these smart contracts by employing the same blockchain technology as `Bitcoin`. Just as Bitcoin's blockchain and network validate Bitcoin ownership, Ethereum's blockchain validates smart contracts, which the encoded rules execute.

Ethereum versus Bitcoin

The main difference between Ethereum and Bitcoin is that Ethereum wants to be the place users go to execute their decentralized applications. In fact, its goal is to be a sort of massive, decentralized computer that executes smart contracts. That's why many other cryptocurrencies can run on the Ethereum platform. The Ethereum blockchain forms a decentralized network where these programs can be executed.

Bitcoin is different in this sense. Its platform gets the miners to compete and solve complicated blockchain math problems. The first one who solves the problem is the winner and gets rewarded. But miners can use Ethereum's platform as a co-working space to create their own products. They get compensated for providing the infrastructure so that inventors can cook their own new types of products.

Ethereum characteristics

Here are some main attributes of Ethereum:

- Ethereum's token symbol for investors is ETH.
- Ethereum is minable.
- Coin creation occurs through proof-of-work (PoW).
- Transaction time can be as little as 14 seconds, although it can go higher based on confirmation requirements.
- Transactions aren't fully anonymous.

- Ethereum is more decentralized than Bitcoin.
- As of 2018, mining Ethereum requires less wasted energy than Bitcoin mining does.

You can find out about different cryptocurrencies' mining profitability at any given time by visiting `www.cryptocompare.com/mining/calculator/ eth?HashingPower=20&HashingUnit=MH%2Fs& PowerConsumption=140&CostPerkWh=0.12& MiningPoolFee=1`.

Ripple

For most of 2018, Ripple was the third largest cryptocurrency by market cap at around $19 billion. However, at the end of 2017 and beginning of January 2018, it temporarily surpassed Ethereum's ranking for ten days.

Some Ripple background

The idea of Ripple actually goes all the way back to 2004. That's way before Satoshi and Bitcoin. In 2004, Ryan Fugger founded a company called RipplePay. According to `https://blog.bitmex.com/the-ripple-story/`, the idea behind the protocol was a "peer-to-peer trust network of financial relations that would replace banks." (If that sounds familiar, that's probably because it's also how blockchain works, as I discuss in Chapter 1).

By 2011, Ripple's target demographic started paying attention to Bitcoin, which was just becoming popular and was doing a better job as a peer-to-peer payment network than Ripple. Ripple's architecture started to shift when an early Bitcoin pioneer, Jed McCaleb, joined the Ripple network in May 2011. Others joined the Ripple bandwagon as time went by.

Finally, Ripple's XRP, a cryptocurrency that also acts as a digital payment network for financial institutions, was released in 2012, according to their website, `https://ripple.com/xrp/`. Like many other cryptocurrencies, XRP is based on a public chain of cryptographic signatures. That being said, Ripple is very different from traditional cryptos like Bitcoin and even Ethereum.

Some people don't consider Ripple a true cryptocurrency. Also, Ripple as a company and Ripple the cryptocurrency are two different things, although they're connected. Ripple the coin, which trades as XRP, is the cryptocurrency used with some of the company's payment systems. Ripple the company does business as Ripple Labs, Inc., and provides global payment solutions for big banks and such using blockchain technology.

Ripple versus Bitcoin

Here are some of the key differences between these two cryptocurrencies:

- **Ownership and decentralization:** Bitcoin is owned by no particular person or entity, and Bitcoin the cryptocurrency is pretty much the same as Bitcoin the open-source platform. That's why Bitcoin is highly decentralized and open source, owned by a community that agrees on changes. This setup can make upgrades tough and is why Bitcoin has had a ton of forks (hard and soft) in its history.

  By contrast, Ripple is a private company called Ripple Labs, with offices all over the world. Ripple's digital asset (cryptocurrency) is called XRP and is also owned by Ripple Labs. The company constantly looks to please everyone (especially its partners) and come up with consensus, which can allow for faster upgrades. It has an amendment system with which the developers seek consensus before making changes to the network. In most cases, if an amendment receives 80 percent support for two weeks, it comes into effect, and all future ledgers must support it. Basically, Ripple is a democracy that tries to avoid hard forks and nasty splits.

 You can find out more about Ripple and its most recent updates at `https://ripple.com/`.

- **Transaction speed and fees:** This area is where Ripple really starts to shine. Bitcoin's transaction speed can sometimes go up to an hour depending on fees. And the fees can reach $40 depending on demand.

  Ripple's transactions, on the other hand, can settle in as little as four seconds. Fee-wise, even when the demand was super high at the end of 2017, Ripple's transaction fees averaged $0.007 — a fraction of that of Bitcoin.

 You can compare different cryptocurrencies' historical transaction fees at `https://bitinfocharts.com/comparison/transactionfees-btc-xrp.html`.

- **Number of transactions per second:** At any given second, you can make around ten Bitcoin transactions. Enter Ripple, and raise the number to 1,500. Although some Bitcoin forks aim to resolve this issue, at the time of writing Ripple appears to be ahead of the game.

- **Coin amount limits:** Bitcoin and other minable cryptocurrencies have finite numbers of coins, which come into the market only through mining. But XRP is limited to the 100 billion coins in circulation now, largely to appeal to Ripple's (the company's) biggest clients, which are large financial institutions.

Ripple characteristics

The following list gives you a summary of Ripple's main features:

- Ripple's token symbol for investors is XRP.
- Ripple's XRP isn't minable — no miners whatsoever.
- Coin creation and algorithm processing happens through consensus, *not* PoW.
- Transaction time can be as little as four seconds.
- Transactions can be made anonymous.

_____

_____

_____

- Ripple isn't fully decentralized.
- Energy cost per transaction is minor.

Because these unique features are so different from Bitcoin's, some people believe Ripple's XRP isn't truly a cryptocurrency. Ripple is actually a strange hybrid of a *fiat currency* (the traditional form of currency backed by a local government, such as the U.S. dollar) and a traditional cryptocurrency. This deviation is because Ripple primarily seeks to serve financial institutions like American Express instead of focusing on the spread of Ripple's XRP among everyday users, at least as of October 2018. This may very well change in the future.

Litecoin

Litecoin has been hovering around the top ten largest cryptocurrencies by market cap since its inception in 2011. Its ranking has gone up as high as number two and dropped as low as number seven, so its market cap has been one of the more volatile ones among celebrity cryptos. As of October 2018, its market cap is around $3 billion, making it the seventh largest cryptocurrency after Bitcoin, Ethereum, Ripple, Bitcoin Cash, EOS, and Stellar.

A little Litecoin background

Litecoin is a result of a Bitcoin hard fork that happened in 2011. It wanted to become the lighter and faster version of Bitcoin. Litecoin was released by Charlie Lee, a Google employee and an MIT graduate. It reached $1 billion market capitalization by November 2013. Check out the Litecoin project here: `https://litecoin.org/`.

If you had invested in Bitcoin end of 2016, it would've grown 2,204 percent by the end of 2017. But if you had invested in Litecoin then, it would've grown over 9,892 percent. Not too shabby.

Litecoin versus Bitcoin

Litecoin's technology isn't *that* different from that of Bitcoin. Lee didn't even want it to compete with Bitcoin; he wanted it to complement Bitcoin, like silver complemented gold in the old days. As the gold of cryptos, Bitcoin is great for buying expensive stuff like houses and cars. That's because Bitcoin may be presumed as more secure than Litecoin, although many crypto enthusiasts insist neither are truly secure. Litecoin, on the other hand, can be used for buying cheap things and day-to-day stuff where security isn't that much of a concern and transaction speed is more important. Here are some other differences between the two:

- **Mining difficulty:** Mining Bitcoin is becoming more difficult and expensive as time goes by. To really make money mining Bitcoin, you need a very powerful computer. You can mine Litecoin, on the other hand, using normal computers.

- **Total number of coins:** Bitcoin has a finite number of 21 million coins. Litecoin can accommodate four times that amount, up to 84 million coins.

- **Transaction speed and fees:** On Bitcoin's network, transaction confirmation time averages around ten minutes and can sometimes take up to an hour. For Litecoin, the speed is roughly 2.5 minutes, according to data from BitInfoCharts.com. Litecoin's transaction fee is also considerably lower than Bitcoin's, averaging less than $0.08. Its highest point until October 2018 was around $1.40 ,when the crypto demand was super high in December 2017.

Litecoin characteristics

Litecoin's main traits include the following:

- Litecoin's token symbol for investors is LTC.
- Litecoin is minable.
- Coin creation and algorithm processing occurs through the proof-of-work (PoW) process.
- Transaction time is around 2.5 minutes.
- Transactions can be made anonymous.
- Litecoin is decentralized.
- Litecoin's energy cost per transaction is lower than Bitcoin's.

Although team Bitcoin and team Litecoin argue their respective cryptocurrencies are the best, at the time of writing neither is a clear winner. The best way to go about your investment strategy may be to diversify your assets not only between these options but also well among the other categories of cryptocurrencies I cover in this chapter. Find out more about diversification in Chapter 3.

Other top ten major cryptos

In the preceding sections, I introduce some of the most well-known cryptocurrencies that also have some of the largest market capitalization on average. But being famous doesn't mean they're necessarily better. In fact, many analysts and investors believe some of these celebrity cryptocurrencies may vanish within ten years. Also, having a bigger market cap doesn't necessarily mean having a brighter future. Their current popularity may just be the proverbial 15 minutes of fame, and they may therefore have lower growth opportunity compared to those that are less known.

Chances are that if anything should happen to a core cryptocurrency, a hard fork may come along that saves it. If you've already invested in a cryptocurrency when it forks, you get the same amount of new coins anyway. That's why I've recommended to my Premium Investing Group members in 2017–2018 to start their cryptocurrency portfolio by first diversifying among the top ten largest ones by market cap and then get into other, different categories. You can stay up-to-date with my most recent cryptocurrency investing strategies here: https://learn.investdiva.com/join-group.

The remaining cryptocurrencies in the top ten keep bouncing on and off the list, but Table 2-1 shows some (in alphabetical order) that were on the list more consistently during 2017 and 2018 and that I personally invested in during 2018.

Crypto	Symbol	Description
Bitcoin Cash (www.bitcoincash.org/)	BCH	A Bitcoin fork that provides cheaper transactions and a more open development process
Cardano (www.cardano.org/en/home)	ADA	Established by a co-founder of Ethereum; smart contracts platform; the "Ethereum of Japan"
Dash (www.dash.org/)	DASH	Digital cash; private transactions via masternodes (computer wallets that host the full copy of the coin's ledger); quick confirmation times and low fees
EOS (https://eos.io/)	EOS	A smart contract platform similar to Ethereum but with performance and scalability benefits
IOTA (www.iota.org/)	MIOTA	No blockchain; instead uses something called Tangle; no mining; no transaction fees
Stellar (Lumens) (www.stellar.org/)	XLM	Similar to Ripple; an open platform for building financial products that connect people everywhere

Table 2-1: *Some Top Ten Cryptos as of 2018*

Top 100 major cryptos

You can dive into the top 100 major cryptocurrencies and still not find *the one* you want to have a long-term relationship with. At this point, selecting cryptocurrencies that match your portfolio really becomes like online dating. You've got to make some decisions based on first impressions and then go on dates (start making small investments and do more research) to discover whether a currency is worthy of a bigger chunk of your crypto portfolio. Table 2-2 lists some options, in alphabetical order, that I've been following on my daily broadcast for NewsBTC.

Crypto	Symbol	Description
Golem (https://golem.network/)	GNT	Worldwide supercomputer network; aims to become the Airbnb for computing, machine learning, and AI
Monero (https://getmonero.org/)	XMR	Famous for anonymous, untraceable, and private transactions
NEM (https://nem.io/)	XEM	The world's first "smart asset" blockchain; built with businesses in mind
NEO (https://neo.org/)	NEO	"Ethereum of China"; aims to become a smart economy platform
OmiseGo (https://omisego.network/)	OMG	Smart contract platform using proof-of-scale based on Ethereum platform that wants to "unbank the banked"

Table 2-2: *Some Top 100 Cryptos as of 2018*

Crypto	Symbol	Description
Populous (https://populous.com/)	PPT	Provides small and medium-sized enterprises an invoice discounting platform on the Ethereum blockchain
SiaCoin (https://sia.tech/)	SC	Decentralized cloud storage platform that uses a blockchain to facilitate payments
TRON (https://tron.network/)	TRX	Decentralized entertainment and content-sharing platform that uses blockchain
VeChain (https://www.vechain.org)	VET	Blockchain-based platform that gives retailers and consumers the ability to determine the quality and authenticity of products they buy
Verge (https://vergecurrency.com/)	XVG	Just like Bitcoin but with faster transactions, aiming to bring blockchain transactions into everyday life through its open-source software

Cryptocurrencies by Category

As an alternative to selecting cryptocurrencies by market cap, the best way to truly diversify your portfolio, for both value and growth purposes, may be to go about selecting cryptocurrencies by category. After you've flipped through the categories and selected the finalists that best fit your risk tolerance, you can then move on to the advanced techniques I discuss in Chapter 5.

Here are some of the most popular cryptocurrency categories and the leading cryptos in each space. I cover these based on their popularity and total market cap as of 2018. The following sections describe just a few examples of many categories in the exciting cryptocurrency world; you may recognize some of the currencies from their coverage earlier in this chapter. Other people may categorize these cryptos differently. Some popular cryptocurrency categories include the following:

- Gaming/gambling
- Supply chain
- Transportation
- Medical
- Internet of Things (IoT)

 Some categories are hotter as of this writing, but others may have become more popular by the time you get this book in your hands. Also know that some cryptos are hybrids of multiple categories and are hard to fit in only one box. You can find different crypto categories on websites such as www.upfolio. com/collections#Go and www.investitin. com/altcoin-list/.

Payment cryptos

Payment cryptos are by far the biggest category in terms of total market cap. In this group, you find cryptocurrencies that mainly aim to be used as a store of value, transaction, and payments, just like fiat currencies like the U.S. dollar. Examples of cryptocurrencies that fall into this category include

- Bitcoin (BTC)
- Litecoin (LTC)
- Bitcoin Cash (BCH)
- OmiseGo (OMG)
- Dash (DASH)
- Ripple (XRP)
- Tether (USDT; https://tether.to/)

Privacy cryptos

Privacy cryptos are heavily focused toward transaction security and anonymity, a lot more than those in the payment category are. In fact, the idea that Bitcoin and other cryptocurrencies in the payment category are fully anonymous and untraceable is a common misconception. Many blockchains only disguise users' identities while leaving behind a public record of all transactions that have occurred on the blockchain. The data in the ledger often includes how many tokens a user has received or sent in historical transactions, as well as the balance of any cryptocurrency in the user's wallet. Here are some examples:

- **Monero (XMR):** Monero is the most famous privacy crypto as of 2018.

- **Zcash (ZEC):** Zcash is similar to Monero but has a different protocol (set of rules). Check it out here: `https://z.cash/`.

- **CloakCoin (CLOAK):** A lesser-known privacy crypto, CloakCoin has a number of added layers of security. See `www.cloakcoin.com/en`.

- **Dash (DASH):** Also mentioned in the payment category, Dash is a bit of hybrid. In addition to Bitcoin's core features, Dash also includes the option for instant and private transactions.

Platform cryptos

Platform cryptos are also referred to as *decentralized application protocol cryptos*, *smart contract cryptos*, or a hybrid of all three. In this category, you can find cryptocurrencies that are built on a centralized blockchain platform; developers use them to build decentralized applications. In other words, such cryptocurrencies act as platforms where people build upon blockchain applications (and thus other cryptocurrencies).

In fact, some analysts suggest you may want to forget about payment cryptocurrencies and invest in crypto platforms instead. They're generally considered good long-term investments because they rise in value as more applications are created on their blockchain. As blockchain technology becomes more mainstream, the number of applications and their usage will increase, along with the price of such coins.

The most famous example in this category is Ethereum (ETH). Others include:

- **NEO (NEO):** A smart contracts ecosystem similar to Ethereum, NEO wants to be a platform for a new smart economy. NEO is China's largest cryptocurrency.

- **Lisk (LSK):** Lisk is a smart contracts platform similar to Ethereum but based on JavaScript. See `https://lisk.io/`.

- **EOS (EOS):** Another smart contracts platform similar to Ethereum, EOS has performance and scalability benefits.

- **Icon (ICX):** Icon wants to "Hyperconnect the World" by building one of the largest decentralized global networks. See `https://m.icon.foundation/?lang=en`.

- **Qtum (QTUM):** Qtum is a Singapore-based Ethereum and Bitcoin hybrid. See `https://qtum.org/`.

- **VeChain (VEN):** VeChain is a blockchain-based platform that gives retailers and consumers the ability to determine the quality and authenticity of products they buy.

- **Ark (ARK):** Ark wants to provide an all-in-one block-chain solution for developers and start-ups. See `https://ark.io/`.

- **Substratum (SUB):** Substratum wants to create a new generation of Internet. See `https://substratum.net/`.

Exchange-specific cryptos

Exchange-specific cryptos are the cryptos that mainly the crypto-currency exchanges introduce and use. You can think of these cryptos as incentives that bring people to the exchanges' platforms. To select the best exchange-specific cryptocurrency, you can consider taking the steps in Chapter 3 to choosing the best cryptocurrency exchange. Here are a few examples:

- **Binance Coin (BNB):** Issued by Binance exchange, Binance Coin runs on the Ethereum platform and has a strict maximum limit of 200 million BNB tokens. See `www.binance.com/`.

- **KuCoin Shares (KCS):** KuCoin Shares is just like Binance Coin but for the KuCoin exchange. See `www.kucoin.com/`.

- **Bibox Token (BIX):** Bibox Token is one of the smaller exchanges that has successfully launched its own token. See www.bibox.com/.

- **COSS Coin (COSS):** COSS Coin is a much smaller exchange than KuCoin, but it's looking to introduce new features as of 2018. See https://coss.io/.

Finance/fintech cryptos

Here I group pure financial cryptos with financial technology (fintech) cryptocurrencies. These cryptos facilitate the creation of a financial system for the blockchain and for people around the world:

- **Ripple (XRP):** Ripple is a blockchain payment system for banks, payment providers, digital asset exchanges, and other companies. It's designed to move large amounts of money quickly and reliably.

- **Stellar Lumens (XLM):** Stellar Lumens aims to develop the world's new financial system. It's building an open system where people of all income levels can access financial services.

- **Populous (PPT):** Populous is a global invoice trading platform to help businesses. Smart contracts automatically perform funding and release payment without a third party.

- **OmiseGo (OMG):** OmiseGo is designed to enable financial services for people without bank accounts. It works worldwide and with both traditional money (fiat currency) and cryptocurrencies.

- **Quoine (QASH):** Quoine wants to solve the liquidity problem in the cryptocurrency market through its LIQUID platform. See `https://quoine.com/`.

- **Bancor (BNT):** Bancor lets you convert between two cryptocurrencies of your choice without another party. See `www.bancor.network/`.

- **Crypto.com (formerly Monaco, MCO):** This cryptocurrency-funded Visa debit card allows you to spend your coins on everyday purchases. See `https://crypto.com/`.

Legal and property cryptos

More cryptocurrencies are emerging in the two categories of legal and property cryptos. But because they're related, I've grouped them together here for now. Here are a couple of examples:

- **Polymath (POLY):** Polymath helps provide legal advice for token investors and smart contract developers. See `https://polymath.network/`.

- **Propy (PRO):** Propy solves problems of purchasing properties across borders when using fiat currencies or cryptocurrencies. It's the first company to ever sell a property on the blockchain and using Bitcoin. See `https://propy.com/`.

Other up-and-coming property cryptocurrencies include REAL and REX, but at the time of writing they're way down on the cryptocurrency market cap ranking list.

_____
_____
_____

3

The Fundamentals of Cryptocurrency Investing

In Chapter 2, I open a window to all the different categories of cryptocurrencies because this whole industry isn't just about Bitcoin or a few other famous cryptos you may have already heard of. Having so many options to choose from is exciting. But having too many options can be tricky. You're always keeping an eye open for the next best thing.

In this chapter, I guide you through the fundamentals of choosing and investing in cryptocurrencies.

Fundamental Analysis for Cryptocurrency Investing

Fundamental analysis is the art of using all the gossip, stories, and facts about a cryptocurrency, its financial situation, and upcoming risk events that may move the market. Here are some methods you can use to pick the best cryptos for you.

Go with what you know

Going with what you know is a golden yet simple method also used in the stock market. If you've already been exposed to certain types of cryptocurrencies or used them in real life and have liked their performance, consider adding them to your portfolio. Say you notice that your favorite online store has added a cryptocurrency payment option to its checkout page and you place an order with it smoothly. That success may be an indication that the trading volume for that cryptocurrency will increase in the future, and the crypto may become a valuable asset for your portfolio.

Choose the right categories

In Chapter 2, I talk about different crypto categories. Certain categories perform better at certain times in the overall market, not just the crypto market. So, for example, if you notice that the financial technology (fintech) sector is heading higher in equities and that everyone is talking about artificial intelligence (AI), you may want to consider browsing through the AI category and finding cryptocurrencies that are involved with it.

Another way to pick the best categories for medium-term investments is to choose from categories that are already outperforming the overall market. I'm not talking about a category that did well just today but rather something that either has been doing well for a few months or even years or is showing signs of picking up. You can pick the hottest category as your top pick and then add on the second and third ones for diversification purposes. I talk more about diversification later in this chapter.

For more-up-to-date information on the hottest cryptocurrency categories, consider joining the Premium Investment group at `https://learn.investdiva.com/join-group`.

The cryptocurrency categories may not always follow the rest of the market. Because cryptocurrency is a very new industry to begin with, you may find opportunities in it that you may not necessarily find in the more traditional equities market. The crypto industry may turn into the safety net if the stock market crashes.

Check out cryptos' websites

Whether you have a number of cryptocurrencies in mind based on your own experience or you've picked a category and now want to choose the best crypto within that sector, you must now start a more detailed analysis on your finalists with the help of their websites. Here are a few ideas to consider.

Flip through their white papers

A *white paper* is something like a business proposal for new cryptocurrencies. It includes everything potential investors need to know about a crypto, such as technology, purpose, financial details, and so on. More-established cryptocurrencies may already have a page that breaks down all this critical information into easy-to-understand video clips and cool infographics on tabs titled "About" or "How It Works." For others, you may just need to find the white paper on the website and try to digest the information by reading. The good news is that white papers are often written in a language that people who aren't experts in the field can understand.

Identify their teams

No one really knows who created Bitcoin, but the rest of the cryptocurrencies out there normally have a team behind them who guide the company and its blockchain technology (see Chapter 1). The team behind the crypto is important even if its platform is completely open source, which means anyone can access and modify it.

When you invest in anything, understanding the background and how it came to life can play a major role. Some things to look for in the management are bios, resumes, and experience in the field. I also like to check the backgrounds of the members of the board of advisors if the company has one. You normally can find such information on the company's website under tabs labeled things like "About Us" or "Our Team."

Browse their partnerships

If you're not willing to take a lot of risk, seeing who in the industry has put their trust in the cryptocurrency you're considering is important. More established cryptocurrencies have been able to team up with traditional giants like IBM and Microsoft and banks like Goldman Sachs. These companies have expert analytic teams perform due diligence before jumping on board with new investments and partnerships. Having reputable partners can be a sign that the company is solid and on the right track to get ahead of the competition.

Another good thing about having partners in the traditional world is that the cryptocurrency may have a higher chance of getting accepted by the masses. If a cryptocurrency has established partnerships with other companies, they are normally listed under a tab named "Our Partners" or "About Us."

Familiarize yourself with their technology

Many cryptocurrencies are tokens from blockchain companies with multiple products. Well-developed websites walk you through their technology and their products in a not-so-intimidating way. The more you get to know the products and the technology behind cryptocurrencies, the easier you can make your decision about the finalists on your list.

Check out their contribution to society

What problems are your shortlist cryptocurrencies trying to solve? Does it matter to you? Are they just here to get rich quick, or do they have a long-term plan for the betterment of society? Finding answers to these questions can help you narrow down your list of finalists. Companies like Ripple describe their social contributions under a subtab called "Ripple for Good." Other companies often use a similar format or simply put their core social contributions first thing on their home page.

Analyze their road maps

Many companies behind cryptocurrencies have sections on their websites dedicated to where they come from, what they've achieved, and what they're planning to accomplish in the future. If available, these road maps are a great way to discover a ton of fundamental information about the crypto in a few minutes.

Get involved

The majority of cryptocurrency platforms love to increase their followings and encourage people to get involved right there on their websites. Depending on the cryptocurrency, getting involved can mean anything from mining (see Chapter 4) to joining its social forums or even starting a new cryptocurrency project on its blockchain platform (like Ethereum). Of course, getting involved also means investing more of your time, so you need to find a balance there.

Cryptocurrency Exchanges and Brokers

After you've familiarized yourself with cryptocurrencies' risks and rewards (see Chapter 1) and have decided that cryptocurrency investing is right for you, you're ready to go crypto shopping. The most popular way to buy cryptocurrencies is to go directly through an online cryptocurrency exchange. However, depending on your cryptocurrency investing goals, you may need to consider alternative methods. In this section, I tell you all about different types of exchanges, brokers, and other cryptocurrency providers.

Note: Regardless of the method you use to purchase cryptocurrencies, you must have a cryptocurrency wallet ready to store your digital assets. Find out more about cryptocurrency wallets later in this chapter.

Crypto exchanges

A *cryptocurrency exchange* is also called a *digital currency exchange,* or DCE for short. It's a web service that can help people exchange their cash into cryptocurrencies and vice versa. Most exchanges are more focused on providing services to help you exchange a cryptocurrency such as Bitcoin into other digital currencies like Ethereum, Litecoin, and so on.

Most exchanges operate online. The most distinguished forms of cryptocurrency exchanges are the following:

- **Centralized cryptocurrency exchange (CEX):** CEXs are similar to traditional stock exchanges. The buyers and sellers come together, and the exchange plays the role of a middleman. These exchanges typically charge a commission to facilitate the transactions made between the buyers and the sellers. In the cryptoworld, *centralize* means "to trust somebody else to handle your money."

  A *crypto/crypto pairing* involves exchanging one crypto-currency (like Bitcoin) for another cryptocurrency (like Ethereum). Some of the most popular central-ized exchanges offering crypto/crypto pairings at the time of writing include Binance (`www.binance.com/?ref=18381915`), Huobi (`www.huobi.com/`), and KuCoin (`www.kucoin.com/#/`).

A *fiat/crypto pairing* involves exchanging a traditional currency (like the U.S. dollar) for a cryptocurrency (like Bitcoin). At the time of writing, some of the most popular centralized exchanges that offer fiat/crypto pairings include Coinbase (`www.coinbase.com/join/59d39a7610351d00d40189f0`), Bittrex (`https://bittrex.com/`), Kraken (`www.kraken.com/`), Gemini (`https://gemini.com/`), Robinhood (`http://share.robinhood.com/kianad1`), and Bitfinex (`www.bitfinex.com/`).

- **Decentralized cryptocurrency exchange (DEX):** A DEX is an exchange that doesn't rely on a middleman to hold your funds. It's a marketplace where buyers and sellers come together and process the transactions directly between one another. In other words, DEXs facilitate peer-to-peer trades.

  Instead of giving your cryptocurrencies to the CEX, you'll give them to an escrow that's centralized by the network running the exchange. Escrow still exists because transactions take as long as five days to clear. As a buyer, you'll have your cash taken out from your account immediately, although the funds aren't moved to the seller's account until the crypto transaction clears. Here are some of the most popular decentralized cryptocurrency exchanges as of 2018: IDEX (`https://idex.market`), Waves DEX (`https://wavesplatform.com/product/dex`), Stellar DEX (`www.stellar.org/developers/guides/concepts/exchange.html`), and Bisq DEX (`https://bisq.network/`).

- **Hybrid cryptocurrency exchange:** Hybrid exchanges are known to be the next-generation crypto trading marketplace. The hybrid approach aims to merge benefits from both centralized and decentralized exchanges to give consumers the best of both worlds. More specifically, hybrids seek to provide the functionality and liquidity of a CEX with the privacy and security of a DEX.

  The first ever hybrid exchange was Qurrex (`https://qurrex.com`), which launched in 2018. Another hybrid cryptocurrency exchange that's gaining attention is NEXT.exchange (`https://next.exchange/`).

Brokers

If you're looking to purchase cryptocurrencies online and invest in them as an asset, cryptocurrency exchanges are the way to go. However, if you're thinking of speculating the price action of cryptocurrencies, you may want to consider brokers.

As cryptocurrencies became more popular, some traditional forex currency brokers started extending their services to cryptos. But keep in mind that the concept of a "broker" doesn't really exist in pure cryptocurrency investing. You can't purchase cryptocurrencies such as Bitcoin through traditional forex brokers. Even though brokers may carry them, all they're really providing is streaming a tradable price on their platform. That way, you may be able to take advantage of the market volatility and make/lose money based on your speculated trading orders.

Traditional forex brokers are market intermediaries who help traders execute trades on their platforms. They're the middlemen between an individual retail trader and networks of big banks. Forex brokers typically get a price from one or multiple banks for a specific currency. They offer you the best price they've received from their banks. You can then trade your favorite currencies based on the prices that are streaming on your broker's platform.

The pros and cons of using a broker

Forex brokers who provide cryptocurrency services have started hardcore marketing to advertise speculative crypto trading. Here are some of the pros and cons of trading through a broker as opposed to using a cryptocurrency exchange:

- **Pro: You get improved liquidity.** Because the brokers get their quotes from multiple exchanges, they're able to provide increased liquidity to customers. That means you have a higher chance of getting your buy/sell orders fulfilled in a timely manner. You also may be able to get a price closer to your initial buy/sell order because the broker has multiple channels to find a buyer and seller to fulfill your order.

- **Pro: You can start trading immediately.** If you go through an exchange, you sometimes need to wait for days before your account is confirmed. With most brokers, the account confirmation can be quicker.

- **Con: You can't invest in cryptos as an asset.** By trading through a broker, you're simply speculating on price volatility of the market. You aren't actually purchasing cryptos or investing in the cryptocurrency market. This distinction means you don't own your cryptos even if you buy them on the brokerage account.

- **Con: You don't have access to wallets.** For the same reason as in the preceding point, no real portfolio or wallet is available for you. This fact also means you can't realize your transfers or cryptocurrency acquisitions.

How to choose a broker

Some rules you need to keep in mind when choosing a broker include the following:

- **Make sure it's regulated.** Each country has strict international regulatory authorities that audit brokers on a regular basis to ensure their security. Your best bet is often to make sure the broker is regulated by two or more regulatory bodies in your country. You can find regulation information on brokers' websites.

- **Consider ease of deposit and withdrawals.** Good brokers will allow you to deposit funds and withdraw your earnings without a hassle. Brokers have no reason to make it hard for you to withdraw your profits because the only reason they hold your funds is to facilitate trading.
- **Beware of promotions.** Some brokers have discovered that people love discount sales, so they use such promotions to attract customers. You must be careful because sometimes brokers use these promotions to push new traders into making risky investments or using unreliable products and signals. That's why you need to do your due diligence and know your broker before you take advantage of a promotion.

One major broker in this field is eToro (`http://partners.etoro.com/A75956_TClick.aspx`). You can also check out Forest Park FX (`https://forestparkfx.com/?id=UU1UckhZSVN3OW1WNnNuNHIxaHlqUT09`). They can help you find a broker suitable for you in your location.

Other methods for buying cryptos

I cover some of the most popular methods to purchase or invest in cryptocurrencies earlier in this chapter. However, these options aren't the only ones, as you find out in this section.

Funds

Many people seek exposure to the cryptocurrency market but don't want to invest in a specific cryptocurrency such as Bitcoin or Ripple. They may be looking for an equivalent of a *mutual fund* or an *exchange traded fund* (ETF), which tracks a basket of different assets such as stocks and indexes (see Chapter 5).

The upside of a fund is that it's somewhat diversified. That's because you get to invest in a number of popular cryptos in one fund, without the hassle of selecting just a few. The downside of most funds is their costs and restrictions.

Credit card

Financial services like Coinmama allow you to buy cryptocurrencies like Bitcoin (BTC), Ethereum (ETH), Litecoin (LTC), Bitcoin Cash (BCH), Cardano (ADA), Qtum (QTUM), and Ethereum Classic (ETC) using a credit card. But they are not available in all countries yet at the time of writing. Check them out here: `http://go.coinmama.com/visit/?bta=53881&nci=5360`.

PayPal

PayPal is a form of online payment system that supports money transfers and serves as an electronic alternative to traditional money. PayPal started out working on Bitcoin integration earlier than many other financial services, back in 2014. However, it then slowed its services down. At the time of writing, you still can't simply send and receive Bitcoins or other forms of cryptocurrencies directly via your PayPal account. However, a few exchanges accept PayPal money transfers, which means you can use PayPal to indirectly buy cryptocurrencies. To do so, you need to choose the third party or a middleman like an exchange or a broker who accepts PayPal payments.

Back in the day, you were able to transfer money to the Coinbase exchange using PayPal. However, at the time of writing, one of the only viable exchanges that accepts PayPal as a form of money transfer is VirWox. One major problem with VirWox is its high fees. If you're looking to trade cryptos through a broker, eToro (`http://partners.etoro.com/A75956_TClick.aspx`) is a famous one that accepts PayPal.

This type of information is constantly subject to change due to cryptocurrencies' volatile current state. The best way to stay on top of cryptocurrency news is on websites such as www.newsbtc.com/ and www.coindesk.com/.

Cash

The process for paying cash to buy cryptocurrencies such as Bitcoin is to find someone who owns cryptocurrencies and is willing to sell them in exchange for cash:

- One place you can find buyers and sellers of crypto-currencies for cash is https://localbitcoins.com/?ch=w7ct. On this website, you can sign up for free, enter the amount you're looking to buy or sell, and choose your preferred payment method — in this case, cash — to find a counterpart.

- Other sites connect buyers and sellers in a way where the seller provides bank details that let the buyer make a cash deposit at the bank. You must keep the receipt to provide proof, and the seller can send you the

Bitcoins. Some options in this vein include `https://www.bitquick.co/` (part of Athena Bitcoin based in Chicago) and `https://paxful.com/` (based in Delaware).

Cryptocurrency ATMs

Cryptocurrency ATMs are becoming more popular. Bitcoin (and other cryptocurrency) ATMs work like any other ATM. The first step in the process is to find one near you, something you can do via a quick online search or at `https://coinatmradar.com/`.

There are several different brands of ATMs with differing methods of verifying your ID and *cryptocurrency address* (a code in your cryptocurrency wallet). Naturally, you need to do some research in finding a secure and trustworthy ATM with a good online reputation. One simple research method is entering the ATM name on Google or Bing and checking whether it has any negative press.

Some cryptocurrency ATMs even provide services to sell digital coins as well as buy. Keep in mind that these types of cryptocurrency machines aren't ATMs in the traditional sense, where they help you connect with your bank account.

Instead, they're machines that are connected to the Internet and direct you to a cryptocurrency exchange in order to provide you with your cryptocurrency.

Diversification in Cryptocurrencies

One of the first things a financial expert tells you when you want to get started with investing is "don't forget to diversify!" You don't want to put all your eggs in one basket, regardless of whether that basket is stocks or cryptos.

When you're building your personal stock portfolio, *diversification* often means having more than one or two stocks. The most conventional diversification method in a personal stock portfolio is to have around 15 to 20 stocks that are spread across different industries. When you diversify among industries, assets, or investment instruments that aren't correlated, you're less likely to see major drops in your portfolio when one of the categories is doing poorly. Diversification doesn't guarantee you have no risk of losses, though. It just reduces that risk if done correctly.

Websites such as https://pro.benzinga. com/?afmc=2f can help you be in the know about the most recent developments across different industries so that you can make better diversification decisions.

You encounter two types of risk in a stock portfolio: unsystematic and systematic. *Unsystematic risk* is the type of risk that you can mitigate by combining multiple industries into one portfolio, but you can't get rid of *systematic risk* simply by diversifying across various industries. Traditional diversification in a stock portfolio helps reduce unsystematic risk. You can't diversify away systematic risk within your stock portfolio, but how about diversifying across other markets?

As we get closer to the next inevitable stock market crash, I think adding unconventional investment instruments such as cryptocurrencies to your portfolio is more important than ever. Here's why: At the time of writing, the cryptocurrency market couldn't be more different from the traditional markets. It's new. It's unregulated, and therefore traditional systematic risks such as political instability or interest rate risks don't really apply to it. In fact, investors may well see cryptocurrencies as a safety net for when things go south in other markets during a major economic crisis.

Long-term diversification

When it comes to adding cryptocurrencies to your portfolio, keep the following two types of long-term diversification in mind: diversifying with non-cryptocurrencies and diversifying among cryptocurrencies.

 For more information on many of the topics in this section, check out these Invest Diva resources:

- The *Forex Coffee Break* education course at https://education.investdiva.com/forex-coffee-break-with-invest-diva-education-course

- My book *Invest Diva's Guide to Making Money in Forex* (McGraw-Hill Education)

- Other service listings at https://learn.investdiva.com/services

Diversification with non-cryptocurrencies

You have so many financial instruments to choose from when you consider diversifying your portfolio across the board. Stocks, forex, precious metals, and bonds are just a few examples. As I explain in Chapter 1, each of these assets has its unique traits. Some assets' inherited risks can offset the risks of the other ones through long-term market ups and downs.

No single golden diversification rule works for all investors. Diversification percentages and the overall mix greatly depend on the individual investor and his or her unique risk tolerance.

The more risk you're willing to take, the higher the chances of a bigger return on investment, and vice versa. If you have a lower risk tolerance, you may consider allocating a bigger portion of your portfolio to bonds and then systematically adding stocks, precious metals, and cryptocurrencies.

Similar to the forex market, you can trade cryptocurrencies versus other currencies. The most common approach at the time of writing is trading them versus a fiat currency, typically the one backed by the country you live in. For example, in the

United States, most people trade Bitcoin versus the U.S. dollar (USD). They don't really think of it as trading these currencies in pairs because it feels a lot like buying a stock. But the fact is that when you buy Bitcoin using the U.S. dollar in hopes of capital gain, you're essentially betting that the value of Bitcoin will move higher against the U.S. dollar in the future. That's why if the U.S. dollar decreases in value at the same time that Bitcoin increases in value, you're likely to make more return on your investment.

This is where diversification can help you reduce your risk. Most cryptos are correlated to Bitcoin in shorter time frames. That's why you can diversify your portfolio with the fiat currencies you trade them against. For example, if you think that at the time you're trading, the U.S. dollar and the Japanese yen aren't correlated, you can open up two Bitcoin trades: one versus the U.S. dollar and one versus the Japanese yen. Of course, to do so, you should make sure your exchange or broker carries these different fiat currencies and offers such trading opportunities.

Note: Speculating the markets carries a lot of risk. It may not be suitable for all investors, and you may end up losing all your investment. Before deciding to trade such assets, you should carefully consider your investment objectives, level of experience, risk tolerance, and risk appetite. Also, you should *not* invest money that you can't afford to lose.

Diversification among cryptocurrencies

The majority of cryptocurrency exchanges offer a wider selection of cross-crypto pairs than they do fiat/crypto pairs. Some exchanges don't even accept any type of fiat currencies altogether. That's why many traders have no choice but to trade one cryptocurrency against another. Bitcoin (BTC) versus Ethereum (ETH) gives you the BTC/ETH pair, for example.

The thousands of different cryptocurrencies available to trade mean the mixes and matches can be endless. Many cryptocurrency exchanges have categorized these mixes by creating different "rooms" where you can trade the majority of the cryptos they carry versus a number of more popular cryptos. For example, the Binance exchange has created four rooms or categories for the main cross-cryptos: Bitcoin (BTC), Ethereum (ETH), Binance Coin (BNB), and Tether (USDT). By clicking on each of these categories, you can trade other cryptos versus the selected quote currency.

When trading currency pairs, fiat or crypto, the best bet is always to pair a strong base currency (the one listed first) versus a weak quote currency (the one listed second) and vice versa. This way, you maximize the chances of that pair moving strongly in the direction you're aiming for.

The reason you diversify your portfolio is to reduce its exposure to risk by including assets that aren't fully correlated. The big problem about diversifying within your cryptocurrency portfolio is that, at least at the time of writing, most cryptocurrencies are heavily correlated to Bitcoin. Most of the days where Bitcoin was having a bad day in 2017 and 2018, the majority of other cryptocurrencies were, too.

This correlation is one key reason short-term trading cryptocurrencies is riskier than many other financial instruments. Considering long-term investments when adding cryptocurrencies to your portfolio may be best. That way, you can reduce your investment risk by diversifying within different crypto categories.

On the bright side, as the cryptocurrency market continues to develop, the diversification methods can also improve, and the whole market may become less correlated to Bitcoin.

_____

_____

_____

Diversification in short-term trades

If you've calculated your risk tolerance and the results are pretty aggressive, you may want to consider trading crypto-currencies in shorter time frames. Here are some suggestions to keep in mind:

- **Beware of commissions.** Cryptocurrency trading exchanges generally require lower commission and transaction fees than brokers who offer forex or stocks. But you shouldn't completely ignore the commission cost to your wallet. When day trading, you may end up paying more in commissions than what you're actually making by trading if you trade way too often, getting in and out of trades way too fast without calculating your returns. Also, cheaper isn't always the best option when choosing an exchange. You always get what you pay for.

- **Keep expanding your portfolio.** Some people invest a lump sum in their investment portfolios and then either wipe it out in dangerous day-trading actions or get stuck in a strategy that's working but isn't maximizing their returns. A healthy portfolio requires nourishment. Consider leaving a monthly investment fund aside out of your paycheck to expand your portfolio and make your money work for you.

- **Observe the rule of three.** You can mix and match crypto/crypto and fiat/crypto pairs like there's no tomorrow if your account size lets you. However, the key in having a healthy diversified portfolio is to avoid double-dipping the same quote currency in your trades. Try to limit your open short-term positions against each quote currency to three. For example, trade one crypto versus Bitcoin, another versus Ethereum, and a third versus your exchange's cryptocurrency. This approach also helps you keep your portfolio at a reasonable size so it's not too big to monitor.

Cryptocurrency Wallets

A *cryptocurrency wallet* is a software program that helps you manage your digital money. Though you may be the type of person who doesn't like to carry around traditional wallets and would rather put your cash and credit cards right in your back pocket, you must have a digital cryptocurrency wallet if you want to use any type of cryptocurrency. Cryptocurrencies aren't stored in a bank reserve like other types of traditional assets such as gold and cash. Without crypto wallets, the whole idea of cryptocurrencies dies. Cryptocurrency wallets are the air that keeps the system alive.

Before you get started, take a look at some geek terms that you may encounter as you explore the world of crypto wallets:

- **Hot wallet:** A wallet connected to the Internet.
- **Cold wallet:** A wallet that isn't connected to the Internet.
- **Wallet address:** A number that functions something like a traditional bank account number.
- **Public key:** A code that allows you to receive cryptocurrencies into your account or wallet. It's mathematically linked to your wallet address, but it isn't identical.
- **Private key:** A code that's coupled with the public key to ensure your security.

How a wallet works

Crypto wallets don't actually store the cryptocurrency itself; rather, they store the cryptocurrency's private and public keys. These keys are something like the PIN code you use to access your bank account.

No two wallet addresses are the same. They're something like fingerprints. This distinction means that there is a very low chance that somebody else can get your funds by mistake. Also, you have no limit to the number of wallet addresses you can create.

To give you an example of what a cryptocurrency address looks like, here is the wallet address believed to belong to the creator of Bitcoin, Satoshi Nakamoto: **1A1zP1eP5QGefi2DMPTfTL5SLmv7DivfNa**

As you can see, it uses a combination of numbers and letters, both uppercase and lowercase. Don't worry; as long as you have a safe and secure wallet, you don't have to memorize your crypto wallet address. Personally, I keep my wallet address and other keys in a locked document on a secure computer. You can also consider printing your keys and storing them somewhere safe that you won't forget about.

A private key does the job of a unique individual password to your individual crypto wallet address. A public key then adds an extra layer of security and ensures that your wallet can't be hacked. Here is a quick example of what the keys look like:

- **Private key:** 03bf350d2821375158a608b51e3e898e507 fe47f2d2e8c774de4a9a7edecf74eda
- **Public key:** 99b1ebcfc11a13df5161aba8160460fe1601d541

These addresses look completely different to the eye, but the software technology knows that the two keys are specifically linked to each other. That proves that you're the owner of the coins and allows you to transfer funds whenever you want.

When someone sends you any type of cryptocurrency, he or she is essentially signing off ownership of those cryptos to your wallet's address. To be able to spend those cryptos and unlock the funds, the private key stored in your wallet must match the public address the currency is assigned to. If the public and private keys match, the balance in your wallet increases, and the sender's balance decreases accordingly. No exchange of real coins actually occurs. The transaction is signified merely by a transaction record on the blockchain (see Chapter 1) and a change in balance in your cryptocurrency wallet.

Different types of wallets

You may already be using digital wallets, also known as e-wallets, through your mobile phone. Personally, I use wallet apps for my train tickets, parking tickets, and Apple Pay (a mobile payment and digital wallet service by Apple Inc. that allows users to make payments in person, in iOS apps).

Cryptocurrency wallets are a whole different animal; furthermore, they come in several different species catering to different needs. The following sections cover the five most popular types of cryptocurrency wallets, in order of their security level (from least secure to most).

Online wallet

Online wallets may be less secure, but they do have a bunch of advantages for small amounts of cryptocurrencies. An *online* (or *web*) *wallet* allows you access to your cryptos via the Internet. Therefore, as long as you're connected to the Internet (the cloud), you can reach and store your coins and make crypto payments. The online wallet provider stores your wallet's private key on its server. The provider may send you the crypto code but store your keys and give you the ability to access your keys. Different services offer various features, with some of them linking to multiple devices such as your mobile phone, tablet, and computer.

Mobile wallet

Mobile wallets (which fall into the category of software wallets) are available on your cellphone through an app. You can use mobile wallets when shopping in physical stores as cryptocurrencies become more acceptable. *Note:* Other types of wallets, such as online wallets (see the preceding section), offer mobile versions as well. But some wallets are specifically and only used for mobile phones.

Desktop wallet

You can download a *desktop wallet* and install it on your computer. Some argue that desktop wallets (which fall into the category of software wallets) are safer if your computer isn't, or even better, has never been connected to the Internet. If a desktop computer has never been connected to the Internet, it essentially becomes a cold wallet. On the other hand, a computer that has never been connected to the Internet may expose you to malware that may automatically move from the wallet drive that you connect to the computer and infect the desktop since it's never been patched with software updates that require an Internet connection. Talk about a catch-22.

To set up your wallet on a computer that has never been connected to the Internet, you must first download the latest version of the wallet on a computer that *is* connected to the Internet. You then move the file to a USB drive or something similar in order to move it to your offline computer.

Hardware wallet

A *hardware wallet* can arguably be one of the safest types of crypto wallets out there. These wallets store your private keys on a device like a USB drive. You're still able to make online transactions, but the wallets are offline most of the time, so you can consider them cold wallets.

For security purposes, a hardware wallet is an absolute must for large crypto amounts. Keeping a ton of your assets on other, less secure types of wallets increases your risk of unrecoverable hacking attacks.

Paper wallet

A *paper wallet* is a super cold crypto wallet. To use it, you print out your private and public keys. You can send funds by transferring the money to the wallet's public address, and you can withdraw or send your currencies by entering your private keys or by scanning the QR code on the paper wallet.

Some paper wallet generators include `Bitaddress.org`, `WalletGenerator.net`, `Bitcoin paperwallet.org`, and Mycelium (`https://mycelium.com/mycelium-entropy.html`). Mycelium offers an original and even more secure way to generate paper wallets, with a USB device that you plug directly into your printer. The device generates a paper wallet that automatically gets printed out without ever having touched your computer.

How to Keep the Losses Down

A phenomenon called *loss aversion* occurs in behavioral finance when investors keep the losing assets in their portfolios while actively selling the "winners." This tendency is why going against the crowd is one way to curtail your losses. The following sections explain some techniques you can use to keep your crypto investing losses down.

Measure returns

Managing your cryptocurrency investments can be challenging because your assets may be scattered over different exchanges and cryptocurrency wallets. Additionally, you may have purchased some altcoins by using Bitcoin, some others by using the U.S. dollar (USD), and more by using cryptos such as Ethereum or Litecoin. That's why I recommend you keep a log of your investments and ink any changes you make to your portfolio. Here are the three steps in determining your portfolio returns:

- Measuring the amount you've invested
- Measuring capital gains, which is the profit you make through buying and selling cryptos
- Measuring income, which is the payment you get by holding some cryptos (if applicable)

To calculate the amount invested, you can create a list like the one in Figure 3-1. The table shows numbers of coins, buying date, cost (both total and per coin), and current value.

My Crypto Portfolio as of September 1, 2018						
Coin	Full name	Number of coins	Date bought	Total cost (including commission) (USD)	Cost per coin (USD)	Current price per coin (USD)
BTC	Bitcoin	0.5	6/29/2018	2,965	5,900	7,155
ETH	Ethereum	8	8/14/2018	2,250	275	293
XLM	Stellar Lumens	200	8/07/2018	44	0.200	0.2257
EOS	EOS	50	8/16/2018	225	4.45	6.55

© John Wiley & Sons, Inc.

Figure 3-1: *An example of a cryptocurrency investment log.*

Because you may be purchasing different coins by using either *fiat* (government-backed) currencies, such as the U.S. dollar, or other cryptocurrencies, you may need to convert your investment value to one type of currency to keep it simple and easier to track. In Figure 3-1, I converted all my purchasing value to the U.S. dollar (USD). Another way to track your investment is to create separate logs depending on how you purchased your altcoins. For example, you can have a separate log for your investments with BTC and another one for those you purchased with USD.

You can create such logs on a monthly, quarterly, or annual basis depending on your investing time frame. For example, if you're a short-term trader, you may need a monthly log. If you're a medium-to-long-term investor, you can use quarterly and annual logs. You can normally find the return on your investment calculated by your brokerage or exchange services (covered earlier in this chapter).

Many crypto enthusiasts have given up measuring returns against fiat currencies like the USD altogether. If you believe Bitcoin is king and Ethereum is queen, you may end up buying most of your altcoins by using the king and queen anyway. Converting your crypto purchase to its USD value can be time-consuming. Also, most of the time you can't cash out in fiat currencies on your exchange anyway. USD, Bitcoin, and Ethereum all have fluctuations of their own versus other currencies, so a conversion may give you a false gain or loss impression. By converting to USD, it may look like you've gained profit on your initial investment, while in reality you may be in a losing position versus Bitcoin.

If you purchased your coins on an exchange by using another cryptocurrency such as Bitcoin, you can find the relevant USD value by searching your coin and the date you purchased it on `https://tradingview.go2cloud.org/aff_c?offer_id=2&aff_id=13497`.

To measure your capital gains and income, you can simply check your account information with your broker or exchange. With cryptocurrency exchanges, your capital gain information is normally under tabs labeled "Wallet" or "Funds." Most exchanges provide the estimated value of your whole account either in Bitcoin or USD. If you have more than one account, you can add up these estimated numbers in your investment log and monitor them on a regular basis.

Monitor exchange fees

To buy and sell cryptocurrencies, you need services like crypto exchanges and brokers. These companies mainly make money through transaction fees. Although I don't recommend choosing an exchange based only on low fees, sometimes fees can become an important decision-making factor, especially for active traders. The fees can get even larger if you're looking to convert a fiat currency to a cryptocurrency like Bitcoin and then send it to another exchange to buy another cryptocurrency by using Bitcoin, and so on. Fees can be the biggest downside to short-term trading strategies for cryptocurrencies.

Here are some tips for keeping your exchange fees minimal while keeping your investment secure:

- Buy your lump-sum major cryptos on more secure exchanges, which may have higher transaction fees. For example, when I need Bitcoin and Ethereum to trade other cryptocurrencies, I buy a large amount of both on an exchange with higher fees that allows using the U.S. dollar.

- For active trading, choose exchanges that offer lower rates for your specific cryptocurrency pair, but make sure to periodically store your profit on a hardware wallet (covered earlier in this chapter).

- Consider active trading with the exchange's native cryptocurrency. It may have a lower transaction fee than trading other cross-cryptos. For example, the Binance exchange offers cheaper trading options for its cryptocurrency, Binance Coin (BNB).

_____

_____

_____

- Always include the transaction fee when calculating your profit to be on top of your game. For example, if you buy 1 Ethereum coin for $200 but you pay $1.50 in transaction fees, you have spent $201.50 for your investment. While this amount doesn't make a great impact for long-term investments, active traders can feel the accumulative fees over time.

Understand the art of getting out

No matter how thoroughly you conduct your research, at times you may find that getting out of a bad investment is better than holding onto it. The following sections give a few of my general strategies when it comes to getting out of an investment.

Don't be greedy

If you're using a technical chart pattern, always set your profit taking limit order at the price level that's consistent with the technique. You may get a feeling that the market will continue going up after your profit target (PT) is triggered, and you may be tempted to readjust your PT prematurely. Sometimes the market will continue to rise. Sometimes it won't. Personally, I prefer to be safe rather than sorry, so I refrain from readjusting the PT orders way too often (unless I have a valid fundamental reason to do so besides just gut feeling).

Take partial profits

You can call me a hoarder, but I can never let go of all my coins (or any other assets, for that matter) all at once. I set up strategic, partial profit taking prices depending on my investment goals and let the markets handle the rest.

For example, if I buy 10 Ethereum coins (ETH) at $200 and I'm looking to take partial profit at key levels, I may sell 2 of my Ethereum coins at $470, sell 2 more at $591, and keep the rest long term. This way, I gain some profit along the way but don't let go of all my coins, so I still feel happy when the Ethereum price continues going up after I sell. Of course, calculating those key levels needs thorough analysis.

 To view more information on my partial profit taking strategies, join my Premium Investing Group at `https://learn.investdiva.com/join-group`.

Let go of bad investments

Every once in a while, you find yourself holding onto a coin that's just not worth it. With worthy long-term investments,

I tend to buy more coins as the price drops, but sometimes the cryptocurrency, its community, and its management simply don't have a future. This point is when reexamining your fundamental analysis (covered earlier in this chapter) becomes important. When it becomes evident that this coin just isn't going to bounce back, you may as well bite the bullet and get out before your losses get bigger. If you're too scared to do so, you can always take losses in parts, using the partial profit method I talk about in the preceding section.

Note: By letting go of your bad investments and taking losses, you may receive tax credits you can use to offset the taxes you must pay on your capital gains. Find out more about taxes later in this chapter.

How to Let the Profits Rise

I deal with two emotions when the markets start to rise. One is regretting not buying more when the prices were down. The other is the temptation to sell and take profit before reaching my carefully analyzed profit target limit order. What I need to keep reminding myself (and my students and fellow investors alike) is that emotions rarely lead to maximizing profit.

At the end of the day, discipline is what makes your bank. The following sections detail some tricks I use to avoid emotional investing.

Buy at the bottom

Being able to purchase at the lowest price every time you invest is highly unlikely. But studying the market psychology and historical price patterns can help you get close. One of my go-to technical analysis tools to identify the bottom is the Ichimoku-Fibonacci combo.

You can use the Ichimoku-Fibonacci combination to gauge crowd psychology and identify key support and resistance levels. (*Support* is a price level where the market has difficulty breaking below; *resistance* is a price level where the market has difficulty breaking above.) For longer-term investing, I generally use the daily chart for Ichimoku analysis. For example, after the price of Ripple's XRP dropped below $0.70 on May 15, 2018, it then broke below the daily Ichimoku cloud. Following the Ichimoku Kinko Hyo's guidelines, I had an indication that the price of XRP may drop further toward key Fibonacci retracement and support levels at $0.57 and $0.47. By conducting this analysis, I was able to set a buy limit order at these levels ahead of time and aim to purchase at lower prices instead of buying immediately. This way you can maximize your profit and lower your net purchasing price.

 Check out Invest Diva's Premium Investing Group where I routinely share my Ichimoku-Fibonacci strategies: `https://learn.investdiva.com/join-group`.

Know that patience is a profitable virtue

"Patience is a profitable virtue" is my main mantra in all the education courses at Invest Diva. My students say repeating this mantra has changed the way they invest and has increased their profit returns by a fair bit. Whenever I feel the adrenaline rushing through my head from looking at a chart, I take a step back. I change the time frame and look at the big picture. I do more fundamental research. Getting nervous is very easy when the markets take a dip and you've invested a bunch of money in an asset. Being patient can often be the ultimate path to making tangible returns.

Identify the peaks

"Buy low and sell high" is the name of the game! Again, you've got to be either Nostradamus or Lucky Luke to take profit at the highest price every time you invest. But if you use historical data and technical chart patterns, you can stack the odds in your favor. For active trading and medium-term investing in the cryptocurrency market, I still find the Ichimoku-Fibonacci combo pretty useful. Other tools include technical chart patterns and key psychological resistance levels.

Using Ripple's XRP as an example, in September 2018 I identified a double bottom chart pattern in the process of formation on the daily chart. A *double bottom* is a popular formation on charts, where the price has difficulty breaking below a support level twice, forming two valley-shaped bottoms. When confirmed, it can be interpreted as a bullish reversal pattern, meaning that the prices may start going up.

Following the double bottom chart pattern guidelines, medium-term investors can expect the market to take profit when the price has moved up from the neckline the same distance from the bottom to the neckline, or the next available Fibonacci retracement levels. To be safe, I normally recommend taking partial profits at each level to distribute risk.

On September 21, XRP reached both levels and then some before dropping back down. A medium-term investor would've taken profit at these levels, while a long-term investor would've stayed in his or her position.

For long-term investors, timing the profit taking can be a bit more challenging. The crypto market is an exciting new investment opportunity that a majority of people are just discovering. Just like with the dot-com bubble, the hype can lead to extreme volatility. You saw the results of the hype in 2017 when Bitcoin price surged over 1,000 percent and Ripple's XRP gained a whopping 36,018 percent. I personally know investors who sold right at the peak and became millionaires and others who bought at the peak and had to sit on their losses until the next surge. In this case, most investors who were able to sell at the peak are those who went against the hype and against the majority of the crowd.

Technical chart patterns such as double bottoms, indicators such as Ichimoku, and going against the crowd don't guarantee optimal results. These items are simply tools that increase the probability of identifying the best price to buy and sell. At the end of the day, you must conduct thorough risk management that applies to your personal financial goals and risk tolerance.

_____

_____

_____

Find peaks and bottoms with a few trading tools

 Here are some cheat sheets of the trading tools I use to identify peaks and bottoms:

- **Bearish reversal chart patterns:** These patterns form on the chart during a period of surging prices and indicate that the market sentiment and price action may turn bearish and start dropping. Find out more at www.investdiva.com/investing-guide/bearish-reversal-patterns-list1/.

- **Bullish reversal chart patterns:** These patterns form during a downtrend and indicate the prices may start to turn bullish and rise. Check out www.investdiva.com/investing-guide/bullish-reversal-patterns-list/.

- **Ichimoku Kinko Hyo:** This Japanese indicator consists of five different moving averages, helping you get a better view of the current market sentiment and predict the future price action. See www.investdiva.com/investing-guide/ichimoku-kinko-hyo-explained/.

_____

_____

_____

The Tax Treatment of Cryptocurrencies

Before the 2017 crypto hype, many people who got into cryptocurrencies (whether through mining or investing) probably didn't even think about its tax implications. But as cryptocurrency investing becomes more mainstream, its taxation guidelines have taken center stage. In this section, I review the basics of cryptocurrency taxation.

Note: Keep in mind that these guidelines are based on the U.S. tax laws as of 2018. Depending on your crypto investment time frame, type of profit, and personal financial situation, you may need to consult with an accountant to get ready for tax day.

Three types of crypto taxes

The tax setup for cryptos is complicated. In most cases, you treat your cryptocurrency assets as property rather than currency. That means you pay capital gain taxes on your cryptocurrency investments. In this case, you don't have any tax obligations until you sell your coins for a profit. But what if you got your coins by mining? Or what if your employer pays you in cryptocurrencies? To make it simple, I've divided crypto taxation obligations into three likely scenarios.

Income taxes

If you've invested in all the expensive equipment I talk about in Chapter 4 and are getting crypto mining rewards as a result, then you may be considered a crypto business owner. You're technically getting paid in cryptos for your business operation, and therefore you're subject to income tax by the Internal Revenue Service (IRS). Needless to say, you're also subject to income tax if you work for a company that pays you in cryptocurrencies.

If you receive mining or income rewards in crypto worth over $400 in one year, you must report it to the IRS. If you've set up a mining operation at your home, you can report your mining income as self-employment income on Schedule C of your tax return. Personally, though, I've set up my mining activity through my Invest Diva business, which helps me get a more generous tax policy when my net income is high. (I talk about minimizing your crypto income tax later in this chapter.)

_____

_____

_____

Always make sure to keep a record of your mining activity and financial statements in case you get audited by the IRS. Also, if you're filing as a business entity, make sure to consult with a tax professional to discover the best options for your particular scenario. Don't worry — you can even claim the accountant fees on your business.

Note: Even as a crypto miner and a business owner, you must understand the basics of cryptocurrency investing. If you sell or trade your cryptocurrencies for other altcoins or any products, then you must pay capital gain taxes as I discuss in the next two sections (depending on whether they're long term or short term). Your mining activity profits often rely on the market value of the cryptocurrency as well as the amount of tax you'll be paying on them.

Long-term capital gain taxes

In Chapter 1 I point to capital gains as one of the main reasons people invest in cryptocurrencies. That's how the IRS categorizes cryptocurrencies as well. Just like owning stocks and real estate, you must pay capital gain taxes after you sell your crypto assets for a profit. If you take a loss, you can lower your tax bill. Now, if you hold your crypto assets for over a year, you often get a better tax rate. This rate is called a *long-term capital gain tax*.

You can calculate your capital gains by doing simple math on the amount you gained or lost after you purchased your cryptos. For example, if you buy one Bitcoin for $5,000 and sell it for $10,000, then you've made $5,000 in capital gains minus the amount you pay for transaction fees.

Short-term capital gain taxes

A *short-term capital gain tax* is very similar to the mining and crypto income tax I mention earlier in this chapter. If you sell or trade your cryptos regularly and hold them less than a year, then your profit or losses may be categorized as income, which often has less favorable tax implications. Even if you don't officially cash out your cryptos, you may still be subject to short-term taxes if you use the cryptocurrency to purchase stuff, whether it's tangible products or other cryptocurrencies.

Active traders who make a few trades every now and then are subject to different tax laws than day traders who trade cryptos for a living. I discuss the difference in the later section "Reduce your trading tax."

How to minimize your crypto taxes

Whether you've earned your crypto as income or have seen capital gains on your assets, the following sections show you some ways to cut the amount you owe the IRS.

Lower your mining income tax

In the United States, you may get a better tax rate if you create a company or a business entity around your mining activities instead of mining as a self-employed individual. By doing so, you can take advantage of the tax breaks business owners get for paying for business-related stuff and get a better tax rate than individuals. Got that high-end computer to mine Bitcoin? Claim it on your business and lower your taxable income. Got your computer set up with mining equipment like the ASICs and expensive GPUs that I talk about in Chapter 4? Paying a ton on electricity when mining? Congrats, you can get a tax break on the rewards you got paid through mining.

That is, of course, if your coins are actually worth something. Even at a personal level, your mining operation can be very profitable, but it also can cost you a ton — way more than its rewards, especially if the crypto market isn't doing very well at the time.

At the time of writing, if your overall net income is more than $60,000, filing as an S corporation, or an LLC that's taxed like an S corporation, may help you. Consult a tax professional for guidance.

You can claim your expenses on your business only if the LLC, C corporation, or S corporation was created prior to earning the income from mining. Anything earned prior to the company formation won't be able to be included under the company for tax purposes.

Reduce your trading tax

Do you consider yourself a day trader? Then you may be eligible to pay way less in taxes than occasional traders. But first you must pass the IRS day-trading test by being able to answer "yes" to these three questions:

• Do you aim to make profit from the daily price changes in the crypto market instead of holding your positions long term or even overnight?

- Do you spend most of your day trading instead of having a full-time day job?
- Do you have a substantial and regular trading pattern and make a ton of trades on a daily basis?

If you qualify as a day trader, you may be able to claim your rewards as a self-employed individual. This designation means you can deduct all your trading-related expenses on Schedule C like any other sole proprietor.

According to finance.zacks.com, your corporation will be taxed based on your profits and losses whether or not it's a one-owner corporation. You can also use the money you make from day trading to pay for your insurance, healthcare, and employee benefits, if you have any.

Tracking your short-term crypto trading activities can be confusing. The industry has a ton of volatility and market fluctuation, and an exploding number of tradable cryptos are available to you 24/7. These situations make monitoring your resources manually almost impossible. Later I introduce some tracking resources you can use for your trading activities.

Bring down your capital gain taxes

If you can't qualify as a day trader (see the preceding section), your best bet to reduce your crypto capital gain taxes is to be a long-term investor. That means holding your assets for over a year. Don't sell, trade, or buy anything with your cryptocurrencies within a year of your purchase.

As I mention earlier in this chapter, capital gain taxes on investments held for more than one year (long term) can be much lower than capital gain taxes on investments held for less than one year (short term). In 2018, long-term capital gains are taxed at 0 percent, 15 percent, or 20 percent, depending on your tax bracket. If you're in the high-income tax bracket, for example, your capital gains tax rate may be 20 percent. Find out more about tax brackets here: www.irs.com/articles/2018-federal-tax-rates-personal-exemptions-and-standard-deductions.

Trading one cryptocurrency for another may put you at risk of paying more taxes. To purchase certain cryptocurrencies at specific crypto exchanges, you have no choice but to convert your cryptos for one another in a shorter time frame, but if you make a huge profit on the initial crypto, you no longer fall into the category of long-term investor. Talk to a tax professional to ensure that you're paying the correct rate.

Check the rate of your state

In the United States, different states have different state tax laws, and some states have better rates than others for specific groups of people or certain industries. Some states like Florida are considered a "retirement haven" because you don't have to pay individual income and death tax, and you also get a ton of asset protection and property tax benefits. When it comes to cryptocurrency investors, certain states like Wyoming have great tax incentives for crypto companies and investors because cryptocurrencies are exempted from property taxation altogether. In 2018, Wyoming became the first state to define cryptocurrencies as an entirely new asset class. Wyoming officials labeled it as the "utility token bill" and passed it into law in March 2018; it was designed to exempt specific crypto-currencies from state money transmission laws.

 As cryptocurrencies become more popular, you can expect more states to create such laws to incentivize businesses and individuals to bring their crypto talents and money there. That's why it's important that you're in the know with the latest developments in the industry. Websites like `https://pro.benzinga.com?afmc=2f` can help you get such information in a timely manner.

How to evaluate taxable income from crypto transactions

At the end of the day, reporting your crypto income and capital gains is on you. You must keep track of all your taxable events, which means every time you sell or trade your crypto assets for other stuff. At the time of writing, the IRS doesn't require third-party reporting for cryptocurrencies (meaning the entities you buy the cryptos from don't have to report the sales), which makes the tracking and reporting more complicated. Here are some points to keep in mind when you're evaluating your crypto activities.

Track your crypto activity

 The crypto market is expanding, and more monitoring resources are becoming available for traders, investors, and miners alike. Here are a few resources you can check out:

_____

_____

_____

- **CoinTracker** (`https://www.cointracker.io/ ?i=eALc6OxcyXpD`): CoinTracker automatically syncs your crypto transactions with a growing list of exchanges such as Coinbase, Kraken, KuCoin, and more to generate tax forms. It also has an online support team.

- **CoinTracking** (`https://cointracking.info?ref= I248132`): CoinTracking analyzes your investment activity and generates a tax report based on your profit and losses.

- **CryptoTrader.tax** (`http://cryptotrader.tax?fp_ ref=behp6`): This website connects you to a list of exchanges such as Coinbase, Binance, Bittrex, and more, and helps you calculate your crypto taxes in a few minutes. It has great online customer support that answers questions immediately.

Handle crypto forks

You can get free coins when a cryptocurrency is *forked* (where a portion of a crypto's community decides to create its own version of the currency). Of course, nothing is completely free, and you're likely required to pay taxes on the additional cryptos you receive through the fork. For example, if you own

Ethereum and it undergoes a hard fork that pays you an equal amount of the new cryptocurrency in addition to your original Ethereum assets, you must pay ordinary taxes on the new free coins as opposed to long-term capital gain tax. You pay these taxes based on the U.S. dollar value of the new cryptocurrency the day you receive it.

The IRS offers little guidance regarding hard forks and taxation. Consult with a tax professional and stay ahead of the game by tracking all your crypto records using professional websites such as `http://cryptotrader.tax?fp_ref=behp6`.

Report international crypto investments

The cryptocurrency market and its rules are constantly evolving. That's why you must remain up-to-date about all your crypto transactions. But even if you invest in cryptocurrencies outside the United States, you must report the activity to the IRS.

At the time of writing, you don't have to report your cryptocurrency on your Foreign Bank Account Report (FBAR). This guideline is based on a 2014 IRS statement that said, "The Financial Crimes Enforcement Network, which issues regulatory guidance pertaining to Reports of Foreign Bank and Financial Accounts (FBARs), is not requiring that digital (or virtual) currency accounts be reported on an FBAR at this time but may consider requiring such accounts to be reported in the future." Make sure you keep up-to-date with the IRS crypto regulations because they're subject to change every year; consult a tax professional. Also keep in mind that not having to report your cryptos on your FBAR doesn't mean you can hide your foreign cryptocurrency activities from the IRS.

It bears repeating: You're responsible for knowing the tax ramifications of your crypto activity. The IRS has been going after cryptocurrency investments inside and outside the United States. It even forced Coinbase to turn over its customer records in 2017. So people who simply didn't know about the crypto tax implications got into trouble alongside those who were trying to hide their crypto investments.

4

Mining Cryptocurrencies

In this chapter, I explore the basics of cryptocurrency mining. All you need to mine cryptocurrencies is access to high-speed Internet and a high-end computer. *Note:* Not all cryptocurrencies require mining. Bitcoin started the mining craze in 2009, setting up the concept of blockchain technology (see Chapter 1). However, many new coins out there can't be mined and use alternative methods to generate value.

How Mining Works in a Nutshell

Bitcoin and other minable cryptocurrencies rely on miners to maintain their network. By solving math problems and providing consent on the validity of transactions, miners support the blockchain network, which will otherwise collapse. For their service to the network, miners are rewarded with newly created cryptocurrencies (such as Bitcoins) and transaction fees.

To really understand mining, you first need to explore the world of blockchain technology in Chapter 1. Here's a quick overview: If you want to help update the *ledger* (transaction record) of a minable cryptocurrency like Bitcoin, all you need to do is to guess a random number that solves a math equation. Of course, you don't want to guess these numbers all by yourself. That's what computers are for. The more powerful your computer is, the more quickly you can solve these math problems and beat the mining crowd. The more you win the guessing game, the more cryptos you receive as a reward.

If all the miners use a relatively similar type of computing power, the laws of probability dictate that the winner isn't likely to be the same miner every time. But if half of the miners have regular commercial computers while the other half use supercomputers, then the participation gets unfair to the favor of the super powerful computers. Some argue that those with supercomputers will win most of the time, if not all the time.

Cryptocurrency networks such as Bitcoin automatically change the difficulty of the math problems depending on how fast miners are solving them. This process is also known as adjusting the difficulty of the proof-of-work (PoW). In the early days of Bitcoin, when miners were just a tiny group of computer junkies, the proof-of-work was very easy to achieve. In fact, when Satoshi Nakamoto released Bitcoin, he/she/it intended it to be mined on computer CPUs. (The true identity of Satoshi is unknown, and I'm adding "it" because there are even discussions that Satoshi could be a government entity.) Satoshi wanted this distributed network to be mined by people around the world using their laptops and personal computers. Back in the day, you were able to solve rather easy guessing games with a simple processor on your computer.

As the mining group got larger, so did the competition. After a bunch of hard-core computer gamers joined the network, they discovered the graphics cards for their gaming computers were much more suitable for mining.

Mining isn't a get-rich-quick scheme. To mine effectively, you need access to pretty sophisticated equipment. First you need to do the math to see whether the initial investment required to set up your mining assets is going to be worth the cryptos you get in return. And even if you choose to mine cryptocurrencies instead of buying them, you're still betting on the fact that their value will increase in the future.

As Bitcoin became more popular, mining it became more popular, and therefore more difficult. To add to the challenge, some companies who saw the potential in Bitcoin value started massive data centers, called *mining farms,* with ranges of high-end computers whose jobs are only to mine Bitcoins. So next time you think about becoming a Bitcoin miner, keep in mind who you're going up against. But don't get disappointed. You do have a way to go about mining: mining pools, which I talk about later in this chapter.

What You Need to Mine

Before getting started with mining, you should set yourself up with a few mining toys. When you've got everything up and running, mining becomes rather easy because everything happens automatically. The only thing left to do is pay your electric bills at the end of each month. Here's a brief to-do list to get you started:

- **Get a crypto wallet (flip to Chapter 3 for details).**
- **Make sure you have a strong Internet connection.**

- **Set up your high-end computer in a cool location.** By *cool*, I literally mean "low temperature" and not "stylish."

- **Select the hardware to use based on the cryptocurrency you want to mine.**

- **If you want to mine solo (not recommended), download the whole cryptocurrency's blockchain.** Be prepared; for mature cryptos, downloading the whole blockchain may take days.

- **Get a mining software package.**

- **Join a mining pool.**

- **Make sure your expenses aren't exceeding your rewards.**

Before you begin: The mining profitability of different cryptos

Some tech junkies mine just for the heck of it, but at the end of the day, most people mine cryptos with profit in mind. But even if you fall in the former group, you may as well get a reward out of your efforts, eh? Mining profitability can change drastically based on cryptocurrency value, mining difficulty, electricity rates, and hardware prices at the time you're setting up your mining system. You can go to websites like www.coinwarz.com to see which cryptos are best to mine at a given time. As of September 2018, for example, that site indicates the most profitable cryptocurrency to mine is Verge (XVG), while Bitcoin is ranked number seven.

Even if mining isn't profitable at the moment, your cryptos can be worth a lot in the future if the coin value surges. By mining cryptos that have low profitability at the moment, you're taking an investment risk. For more on risk, flip to Chapter 1.

Mining hardware

Different types of cryptocurrencies may require different types of hardware for best mining results. For example, hardware (such as ASICs, which stands for *application-specific integrated circuits*) has been customized to optimize cryptocurrencies like Bitcoin and Bitcoin Cash. But for cryptocurrencies without dedicated hardware, such as Ethereum, Zcash, and Bitcoin Gold, graphics processing units (GPUs) are good enough to process the transactions. Of course, GPUs are still slow at mining compared to mining farms. If you decide to mine Bitcoin with a GPU, for example, you may wait years before you can mine one Bitcoin. You can find GPUs at any store that sells computer hardware equipment.

As mining became more difficult, crafty coders started exploiting graphics cards because those provided more *hashing power*, which is the rate at which you mine. They wrote mining software (in other words, developed mining algorithms) optimized for the processing power of GPUs to mine way more quickly than central processing units (CPUs). These types of graphics cards are faster, but they still use more electricity and generate a lot of heat. That's when miners decided to switch to something called an *application-specific integrated circuit*, or ASIC. The ASIC technology has made Bitcoin mining much faster while using less power. (You can search "where to buy ASIC miner" on your favorite search engine.)

During crypto hype, mining equipment such as ASICs becomes incredibly expensive. At the beginning of 2018, for example, they were priced at over $9,000 due to high demand. That's why you must consider your return on investment before getting yourself involved in mining; sometimes simply buying cryptocurrencies makes more sense than mining them does.

Cryptocurrency mining may make more sense to do in winter because it generates so much heat in the hardware. You may be able to reduce the cost of your electricity bill by using nature as your computer's natural cooling system — or using your computer as your home's heating system. Of course, the cost of the electricity used by mining computers far exceeds the cost of heating or cooling the house.

Mining software

Mining software handles the actual mining process. If you're a solo miner, the software connects your machine to the blockchain to become a mining node or a miner. If you mine with a pool (see the next section), the software connects you to the mining pool. The main job of the software is to deliver the mining hardware's work to the rest of the network and to receive completed work from the other miners on the network. It also shows statistics such as the speed of your miner and fan, your hash rate, and the temperature.

Again, you must search for the best software at the time you're ready to start. Here are some popular ones at the time of writing:

- **CGminer:** CGminer is one of the oldest and most popular examples of Bitcoin mining software. You can use it for pools like Cryptominers to mine different altcoins. It supports ASICs and GPUs.

- **Ethminer:** Ethminer is the most popular software to mine Ethereum. It supports GPU hardware such as Nvidia and AMD.

- **XMR Stak:** XMR Stak can mine cryptocurrencies like Monero and Aeon. It supports CPU and GPU hardware.

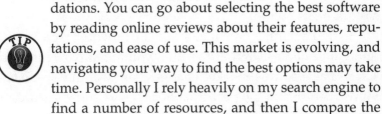

These options are just examples and not recommendations. You can go about selecting the best software by reading online reviews about their features, reputations, and ease of use. This market is evolving, and navigating your way to find the best options may take time. Personally I rely heavily on my search engine to find a number of resources, and then I compare the results to choose the one I feel most comfortable with.

Mining pools

Mining pools definitely bring miners together, but luckily you don't have to get into your beach body shape to join one. Simply put, a *mining pool* is a place where regular miners who don't have access to gigantic mining farms (described earlier in this chapter) come together and share their resources. When you join a mining pool, you're able to find solutions for the math problems faster than going about it solo. You're rewarded in proportion to the amount of work you provide.

Mining pools are cool because they smooth out rewards and make them more predictable. Without a mining pool, you receive a mining payout only if you find a block on your own. That's why I don't recommend solo mining; your hardware's hash rate is very unlikely to be anywhere near enough to find a block on its own.

To find a mining pool that's suitable for you, I recommend doing an online search at the time you're ready to jump in. That's because this market changes rapidly, and so do the infrastructure and the participants. Here are some features to compare when selecting the best mining pool for you:

- **Minable cryptocurrency:** Make sure the pool is mining the cryptocurrency you've selected.

- **Location:** Some pools don't have servers in all countries. Make sure the one you choose is available in your country.

- **Reputation:** This factor is an important one. Don't get in the pool with nasty people.

- **Fees:** Some pools have higher fees than others. Make sure you don't prioritize fees over reputation, though.

- **Profit sharing:** Different pools have different rules for profit sharing. One thing to consider is how much of the coin you need to mine before the pool pays you out.

- **Ease of use:** If you're not tech-savvy, this feature can be important to keep in mind.

How to make sure mining is worth your time

After you have all your tools together, you then need to set up and start mining. It can certainly be challenging to do so, and the dynamic of the mining community changes regularly, so you must make sure that you are up-to-date with recent changes and have acquired the latest tools for your mining adventure.

_____

_____

_____

You can always do so by researching the key elements I mention in the previous sections on your search engine.

If you're looking to mine Bitcoin, keep in mind that your profitability depends on many factors (such as your computing power, electricity costs, pool fees, and the Bitcoin's value at the time of mining), and chances are very high that you won't be profitable at all. You can check whether Bitcoin mining is going to profitable for you by using a Bitcoin mining calculator (check out www.investdiva.com/mining-calculator/). Mining calculators take into account all the relevant costs you may be paying to mine and show you if mining a certain cryptocurrency is profitable for your situation. Simple mining calculators ask you questions about your hash rate, the pool fees, and your power usage, among others. Figure 4-1 shows you a sample mining calculator powered by CryptoRival. Once you hit the "Calculate" button, it shows you your gross earning per year, month, and day.

Source: CryptoRival.com

Figure 4-1: *Example of a simple mining calculator.*

By doing the mining calculation ahead of time, you may realize that mining other cryptocurrencies may make more sense.

5

Trading, Strategies, and the Future of Cryptocurrencies

This chapter introduces you to a variety of cryptocurrency investing techniques like short-term trading, long-term investing, initial coin offerings (ICOs), stocks, and exchange traded funds (ETFs).

Short-Term Trading

Short-term trading can also be called aggressive trading. Why? Because you're taking more risk in the hope of making more profit. Investment of any kind requires a constant balancing and trade-off between risk and return. To earn more return, you must take more risk. When aiming to make money in the short term, you must be prepared to lose your investment (and maybe even more) in that time frame as well, especially in a volatile market like cryptocurrencies.

Short-term trading can be divided into different categories within itself based on how quickly you realize the profits — hours, days, or weeks. Generally speaking, the shorter the trading time frame, the higher the risk involved with that trade.

Hours

If you've ever wondered what a day trader does, this is it. *Day trading* is one form of aggressive short-term trading. You aim to buy and sell cryptos within a day and take profit before you go to bed. In traditional markets like the stock market, a trading day often ends at 4:30 p.m. local time. But the cryptocurrency market runs 24/7, so you can define your day-trading hours to fit your schedule. With this great power comes great responsibility, though.

Here are a few questions to ask yourself to determine whether day trading is indeed the right crypto route for you:

- Do you have the time to dedicate to day trading? If you have a full-time job and can't stick to your screen all day, day trading probably isn't right for you. Make sure you don't use your company time for trading; not only you could get fired, but you also won't be able to dedicate the required time and energy to trading either. Double the trouble.

- Do you have sufficient risk tolerance for day trading? Check out Chapter 1 for more on risks, and attend this webinar to calculate your risk tolerance: `https://learn.investdiva.com/free-webinar-3-secrets-to-making-your-money-work-for-you`.

- Even if you can financially afford to potentially lose money day trading, are you willing to do so? Do you have the stomach to see your portfolio go up and down on a daily basis? If not, perhaps day trading isn't right for you.

If you've made up your mind that day trading is the right crypto route for you, the following sections share some tips to keep in mind before getting started.

Define crypto trading sessions

Because cryptocurrencies are traded internationally without borders, one way you can define a trading day is to go by the trading sessions in financial capitals of the world like New York, Tokyo, the *eurozone* (made up of the European countries whose official currency is the euro), and Australia.

Some sessions may provide better trading opportunities if the cryptocurrency you're planning to trade has higher volume or volatility in that time frame. For example, a cryptocurrency based in China, such as NEO, may see more trading volume during the Asian session.

Know that day trading cryptos is different from day trading other assets

When day trading traditional financial assets such as stocks or forex (the foreign exchange market), you can follow already established fundamental market-movers such as a company's upcoming earnings report or a country's interest rate decision. The cryptocurrency market, for the most part, doesn't have a developed risk-event calendar. That's why conducting fundamental analysis (see Chapter 3) to develop a day-trading strategy is way harder for cryptos.

Set a time aside

Depending on your personal schedule, you may want to consider scheduling a specific time of the day to focus on your trades. The idea of being able to trade around the clock is pretty cool in theory. You can just get on your trading app during a sleepless night and start trading. But this flexibility can backfire when you start losing sleep over it. Remaining alert during day trading, or night trading for that matter, is very important because you need to develop strategies, identify trading opportunities, and manage your risk multiple times throughout the trading session. For many people, having a concrete discipline pays off.

Start small

Day trading involves a lot of risk. So until you get the hang of it, start with a small amount and gradually increase your capital as you gain experience. Some brokers even let you start trading with a minimum of $50.

Note: If you start trading small, make sure you aren't using margin or leverage to increase your trading power. Leverage is one of those incredibly risky tools that's projected as an opportunity. It lets you manage a bigger account with a small initial investment by borrowing the rest from your broker. If you're trying to test the waters by starting small, using leverage will defeat that purpose.

Don't take too much risk

According to Investopedia, most successful day traders don't stake much of their account — 2 percent of it, max — with each trade. If you have a $10,000 trading account and are willing to risk 1 percent of your capital on each trade, your maximum loss per trade is $100 (0.01 multiplied by $10,000). So you must make sure that you have that money set aside for potential losses, and that you aren't taking more risk than you can afford.

Secure your crypto wallet

One major problem with day trading cryptocurrencies is securing your crypto wallet. The least secure cryptocurrency wallets are online wallets (described in Chapter 3). Because you're going to need your capital handy throughout the trading day, you may have no choice but to leave your assets on your exchange's online wallet, which can expose you to risk of hacking.

_____

_____

_____

One way to enhance your security here is to not actually buy and sell cryptocurrencies but rather to speculate the price action and crypto market movements by using brokers who facilitate such services, as I discuss in Chapter 3.

Stay away from scalping

Scalping is the shortest-term trading strategy some individual traders choose. It basically means jumping in and out of trades frequently, sometimes in a matter of seconds. If you're paying commission fees for every trade, not only are you exposing yourself to a ton of market risk when scalping, but you can also get burned out by the fees before you make any profit. Individual traders rarely make any profit scalping.

Days

If you want to trade short term but don't want to stick to your computer all the time, this time frame may be the right one for you. In traditional trading, traders who hold their positions overnight are categorized as *swing traders.* The most common trading strategy for swing traders is *range trading,* where instead of riding up a trend, you look for a crypto whose price has been bouncing up and down within two prices. The idea is to buy at the bottom of the range and sell at the top. If you're using a broker who facilitates short-selling services, you can also go the other direction.

 To identify a range, you must be proficient in technical analysis. A number of technical chart patterns and indicators can help you identify a range. For more on technical analysis, check out my award-winning trading courses at https://learn.investdiva.com/services.

If you choose swing trading rather than day trading, one downside is that you may not be able to get an optimized tax rate that's created for day traders in some countries. In fact, swing trading is in the gray area for taxation because if you hold your positions for more than a year (long-term investing, covered later in this chapter), you also get an optimized tax rate. For more on taxes, flip to Chapter 3.

 If you're trading the cryptocurrency market movements without actually buying them, make sure you aren't paying a ton of commission fees for holding your positions overnight. Consult with your broker before developing your swing-trading strategy, or check `https://forest parkfx.com/?id=UU1UckhZSVN3OW1WNnNuNHIx aHlqUT09` to select a broker that suites your strategy.

Weeks

This time frame falls into the category of *position trading* in traditional markets. Still shorter than a long-term investing strategy but longer than day trading and swing trading, this type of short-term trading can be considered the least risky form of short-term trading. But it's still risky. (Flip to Chapter 1 to read more about risks involved in trading cryptocurrencies.)

For this type of trade, you can identify a market trend and ride it up or down until the price hits a resistance level or a support level. A *resistance* level is a psychological market barrier that prevents the price from going higher. A *support* level is the opposite: a price at which the market has difficulty "breaking below."

To hold your positions for weeks, you need to keep your crypto assets in your exchange's online wallet (see Chapter 3), which may expose you to additional security risk. You may be better off utilizing a broker that provides price-speculation services for this type of trading strategy so you don't have to own the cryptocurrencies.

One popular position-trading strategy involves the following steps: Identify a trend (using technical analysis), wait for a pullback, buy at the pullback within the uptrend, and take profit (sell) at a resistance.

 In my Premium Investing Group, I often provide position-trading strategies for members by using the Ichimoku Kinko Hyo + Fibonacci combo technique. Visit here to join the group: `https://learn.investdiva.com/join-group`.

Long-Term Investing

Do you know how long the first Bitcoin investors waited to see any type of return? Around seven years. Some Bitcoin miners and early investors actually forgot about their crypto assets and had to go on a treasure hunt to find their Bitcoin wallets during the 2017 bubble.

The point is that just like many other markets, time and patience can be your best friends. But you still need to have a plan based on your risk tolerance and financial goals in order to profit long term. In this section, I go over the basics of long-term investing in cryptocurrencies.

How to get started

When I talk about long-term investment strategies, I'm basically treating cryptocurrencies as assets. And just like any other type of financial investment, you need to create a portfolio that goes along with your risk tolerance and financial goals. To do so, you can begin by examining the criteria for constructing your crypto portfolio (such as risk management) and then use them to develop a plan for allocating different types of crypto assets in the categories I explore in Chapter 2. In the following sections, I dig into a couple of things to keep in mind when getting started with your portfolio management.

Your personal goals and current situation

You should consider a variety of issues when managing your portfolio long term. Factors like risk and return are some of the obvious ones that I cover in Chapter 1. But when it comes to long-term investment in risky assets like cryptocurrencies, you need to take it a step further. Here are some questions you should answer:

- What's your income size now, and where can it go in the future?
- Are you likely to change your job in the future? Is your current job secure?
- What's your marital status now? Do you have any children? Where do you see yourself on this front in five years?
- What's your investment experience?
- Do you have any other investments in assets such as equities or real estate? How diversified is your overall portfolio?

These questions may sound cliché, and you may already have the answers in your head. But investing long term is a logical process, and actually writing down the most basic elements of your personal goals and characteristics always pays off. When you've assessed your own financial situation and goals, you can have a better understanding of how

_____

_____

_____

to move forward with your crypto portfolio. Your needs may even determine the avenue you choose.

For example, if you're retired and your income depends on your portfolio, long-term cryptocurrency investing may not be suitable for you. You may want to consider a lower-risk, current-income-oriented approach. If you're young and willing to take the risk in the hope of getting high returns, you may even consider the short-term trading strategies I cover earlier in this chapter.

To sum it up, build your portfolio around your needs depending on the following variables: your current income, your age, the size of your family, and your risk preferences.

 For more on risk management and calculating your risk tolerance, check out this free master class: `https://learn.investdiva.com/free-` `webinar-3-secrets-to-making-your-money-` `work-for-you`.

Your portfolio's objectives

Assessing your personal goals and life situation brings you one step closer to creating your own portfolio (see the preceding section). When creating a long-term portfolio, you generally want to consider these objectives:

- **Generating current income:** These investments can generate a regular payment, which could be at odds with high capital appreciations.

- **Preserving capital:** This low-risk, conservative investment strategy generates moderate returns.

- **Growing capital:** Focusing on capital growth requires you to increase your risk tolerance and reduce your need for a current-income-based investment strategy.

- **Reducing taxes:** If you're in a high tax bracket, you may consider a portfolio that generates capital gains. If you're in a lower tax bracket, you have lower incentive to defer taxes and earn high investment returns, so a portfolio with higher-current-income assets may be suitable for you.

- **Managing risk:** You should always consider the risk-return trade-off in all investment decisions.

These objectives get tied together with your personal goals and other investments. For example, current income and capital preservation are good objectives for someone with a low risk tolerance who has a conservative personality. If you have medium risk tolerance and don't need to depend on your investment for current income as much, you can select capital growth as your portfolio objective. In many countries, including the United States, taxes (see Chapter 3) also play a major role in your investment goals. For example, if you're in a high tax bracket, focusing on capital gains may be a better option for you because you can defer taxes. Last but not least, you should consider your risk-return trade-off in all your investment decisions, whether long term or not.

How to create long-term strategies

Any type of investment can be summed up in four words: Buy low, sell high. But of course no one can get it perfectly right every time. With cryptocurrencies in particular, the market is still testing out new psychological levels, so predicting the highs and lows can be that much more difficult. The following sections introduce some methods to expand your long-term cryptocurrency portfolio.

Observe psychological levels

In 2018 the crypto market still isn't mature enough to enable thorough long-term technical analysis. Besides Bitcoin, many cryptocurrencies are so new that they haven't even formed a full cycle on the trading charts. But as time goes by, key psychological support and resistance levels have started to develop.

The reason psychological levels are already appearing in the crypto market may be that many crypto investors are using traditional technical analysis methods for their cryptocurrency investment strategies. With that, you can expect the crypto crowd psychology to form similar chart patterns to those of other markets, such as equities and the foreign exchange market (forex), in longer time frames like weekly and monthly charts. Crowd psychology is the constant battle between the sellers (the bears) and the buyers (the bulls) in the market that leads to price movements in an asset. Psychological levels are those that the prices have difficulty breaking, due to the strength or weakness of the bears and bulls in the market.

You can find a great deal about investing crowd psychology in plain (and funny) videos in my *Forex Coffee Break* education course at https://learn. investdiva.com/forex-coffee-break-with-invest-diva-education-course.

_____

_____

_____

After you identify the psychological levels, you can use them to develop different types of strategies based on your current portfolio, your risk tolerance, and your financial goals. Here are some examples:

- Buy at a key support level and sell at a key resistance level.

- Buy at current market price and sell at a key resistance level.

- Wait for a pullback when the price reaches a key resistance level and buy lower. Then sell at the next key resistance level.

- Buy at a key support level and hold long term.

Sell when you reach your goal

A cryptocurrency's price may continue going higher after it reaches a key resistance level. But how long do you wait? Which resistance level do you choose? Does using resistance levels even make sense for your financial goals? One realistic way to approach your investment strategy is to sell when you've reached your investment goal. The key here is that you shouldn't look back and regret your decision after you've made the sale, even if the price continues going up after you sell.

Markets may continue to go up after you sell. Don't let your emotions take over your logical decision to sell. If you need the money and have already achieved your investment goal, you have no reason to regret an early sale. If anything, you can always get back in the market with a brand-new investment strategy.

Keep tax consequences in mind

Tax laws change all the time, and they vary in different countries. However, in most cases taxes affect nearly all investment actions. As of 2018, in the United States a maximum of $3,000 of capital losses in excess of capital gains can be written off against other income in any one year. If you have a loss position in an investment and have concluded that selling it is wise, the best time to sell is when you have a capital gain against which you can apply the loss.

Before starting to invest, you must understand the basics of taxes in your country. Flip to Chapter 3 for an overview of how you should consider taxes before making investment decisions.

_____

_____

_____

Initial Coin Offerings

Initial coin offerings (ICOs) are something like fundraising for a new start-up, except that your new idea revolves around a new cryptocurrency rather than a business idea or product. You're trying to raise "money" in the form of other, already established cryptocurrencies such as Bitcoin and Ethereum. In other words, an ICO is crowdfunding, using other cryptocurrencies, for a new cryptocurrency that's (hopefully) connected to an awesome product. The following sections provide the basics on ICOs.

How an ICO works and how to start one

Simply put, an ICO works exactly how start-up fundraising works. You come up with a cool idea for a cryptocurrency. The cryptocurrency may be used for an existing product, or perhaps you have an idea for a product that can work well with a brand-new crypto.

As an example, say a fashion website in New York City showcases display windows in real time. (Okay, this is actually my friend Jon Harari's website, WindowsWear — check out

www.windowswear.com. I've been trying to pitch him the
ICO idea, but he doesn't really understand how it could work
for his business.) But for the sake of argument, say that Jon
decides he wants to change his business strategy, make his
website available to the masses, and let people shop on his
app using WindowsWear's very own digital currency. Call this
brand-new crypto WEAR Coin. But unless Jon is a millionaire
who wants to spend all his money on this idea, he needs to
raise money to make this new cryptocurrency a reality. He can
go to a venture capitalist, a bank, or angel investors and ask
for money. The problem with that approach is that he'll most
likely have to give up part of his ownership of his company.
So instead, he can listen to his friend Kiana and go for an ICO.

Here are the general steps of initiating an ICO:

1. **Create a white paper.**

   A *white paper* is a detailed document explaining a business model and the reason a particular coin may really
   take off. The more use cases Jon has in his white paper
   for WEAR Coin to show it can actually become a popular and high-volume coin, the better.

2. **Add a tab to your website dedicated to ICO funding.**

   In this example, Jon puts a tab on his WindowsWear
   site dedicated to WEAR Coin ICO funding.

3. **Spread the word to your connections and ask for funding.**

4. **Sell a quantity of your crowdfunded coin in the form of *tokens*, which means digital assets.**

   Normally ICOs ask for Bitcoin or Ethereum in exchange for the tokens. But you can also accept *fiat* (traditional government-backed) currencies such as the U.S. dollar.

5. **Send the investors coin tokens.**

   In this example, Jon sends his investors WEAR Coin tokens.

If WEAR Coin really hits, starts getting used a lot, and is listed on a ton of crypto exchanges, the early investors can see a significant return on their investments.

People who invest in ICOs normally don't have any guarantee that the new cryptocurrency will increase in value in the future. Some ICO investments have been incredibly profitable in the past, but future ICOs may not be. Unless you really trust the management, the company's dedication to success, and its knowledge of the business model and the industry, investing in an ICO is very much comparable to gambling. Flip to the next section for more details.

_____

_____

_____

How to invest in an ICO

ICO investing involves a lot of risk. You shouldn't invest money you can't afford to lose in an ICO. If your risk tolerance is low, you can consider many alternative investment assets, as I overview in Chapter 1.

Note also that some ICOs aren't even meant to be investments. They're a tool you can use for a specific product. In the real estate sector, for example, you can use the Propy token to buy properties internationally.

But this is an investing chapter in an investing book, and perhaps you've decided to give investing in an ICO a try. Here are some tips on how you can go about it.

Find ICO listings

You may find out about upcoming ICOs through word of mouth, at a financial event, or through an online ad. If you don't have any specific ICO in mind and just want to search for one from scratch, you can get help from ICO listing websites. But finding the right ICO listing website can be a challenge because more than 100 of them are already out there, and more are popping up every day.

_____

_____

_____

Trading, Strategies, and the Future of Cryptocurrencies

Here are some tips to keep in mind when searching for an ICO listing website:

- Start out by comparing two or three ICO listing websites at a time. Are they all featuring the same ICOs on top? This strategy can help you figure out which website is giving you the verified ICO listing.
- Make sure a site has features such as an ICO calendar, ICO ratings, and ICO descriptions.
- Offering market statistics about the ICO, filters, and scam warning features is a plus.

At the end of the day, using your everyday search engine may be your best bet to find an ICO listing website. You can consider search terms like "ICO listings," "top ICOs 2019," or "best ICO listing websites." Here are a few to get you started:

- Coinschedule: www.coinschedule.com
- ICO Market Data: www.icomarketdata.com/
- ICObench: https://icobench.com/
- ICOindex: https://icoindex.com/

Analyze ICO listings

After you pick your ICO listing website, you're now ready to
evaluate and choose the upcoming ICOs you're interested in
investing in. With hundreds of ICOs popping out every month,
this step can be lengthy, but it's a crucial process. The following list gives you some research points to keep in mind:

- **Who's behind the ICO?** The team of developers and
  management behind the ICO is the most important
  thing you need to find out about. Who are they? What
  are their credentials? The ICO website should give you
  background on the team; otherwise, I would move
  on to the next ICO listing that provides such crucial
  information readily on its website. Try to find the team
  members on LinkedIn to verify their backgrounds (or
  even existence). In addition, try finding ICOs' boards
  of advisors and financial backers. Are these people
  you can trust your money with? Are they dedicated
  to taking their idea to the next step?

  Note: I've been to many ICO pitching conferences
  where the team just kept on name-dropping — things
  like "the prince of Dubai is investing millions in us"

or other unverifiable blabs. In these cases, I normally run, not walk, and never look back.

• **What's the cryptocurrency for?** You want to familiarize yourself with the idea behind the crypto as much as possible. Sure, anyone can start a cryptocurrency and list an ICO. The question is why these people have chosen to do so. What specific value does their token have that other cryptocurrencies already in existence don't offer? Who's their competition? How are they better than the competition? What type of technology are they using? Who is their target market, and how large is it?

Note: Beware of unrealistic promises. Scam projects often make bold claims about their products but have nothing new or disruptive in their technology. If someone claims a new cryptocurrency will replace Bitcoin, end world poverty within a year, fix global warming, or increase in value by 10,000 percent, you can add that project to your scam list.

• **Does the team have a prototype or a code?** You don't necessarily have to have a prototype to launch an ICO. But those with a minimum viable product can show you that the team is serious about the idea and is able to hit future milestones. If a project has no working code whatsoever prior to an ICO, that's a major red flag.

- **Does the team have a blockchain?** The majority of ICOs don't have a blockchain (see Chapter 1). The founders simply pitch the idea for the utility their tokens can provide. Personally, I prefer to search among those that are based on solid blockchain technology that solves a solid problem rather than those that are glorified apps that can be built without creating a brand-new cryptocurrency.

- **What's the plan to drive prices higher after the ICO?** The main reason you invest in an ICO is in speculation that its price will go higher in the future. That's why the team behind the ICO should provide you with a road map on how it's planning to do so. This part of the analysis can be similar to that of any already-trading cryptocurrency I talk about in Chapter 2.

Many teams seek to create their own exchanges in order to generate the liquidity and volume needed to take off. But I wouldn't view that as sufficient evidence for the token's future success. Getting listed on various exchanges can be tough, which is why it's an important indicator of the token's success down the road.

- **Does the team have a wide, supportive community?** You don't want to be a sheep who simply follows others, but reaching out to the ICO community can give you a sense about the token. How many supporters does a given ICO have on sources like Reddit, Twitter, and Facebook? Do the supporters appear to be robots, or are they real people and crypto enthusiasts? Beware of paid "community members" whose job is to say positive things about the ICO on social media. Also look for proper media coverage, press releases, and the team's presence on the social media.

Buy into the ICO

When you've found your unicorn ICO, you normally need to have a legit cryptocurrency to invest in it, although sometimes ICOs accept fiat currencies as well. Most importantly, you also need to have a cryptocurrency wallet (see Chapter 3).

_____

_____

_____

Most ICOs are built on the Ethereum blockchain. That's why in many cases you specifically need Ethereum cryptocurrency and an Ethereum wallet to invest in an ICO. See Chapter 2 for more about this crypto.

Not all ICOs are created the same. Therefore, I can't show you the exact steps to take when buying into an ICO. Regardless, here are some general guidelines:

1. Make sure you check the official page of the ICO.

2. If the ICO requires you to pay by another crypto, such as Ethereum or Bitcoin, you must first acquire those coins on an exchange and store them in your crypto wallet.

3. After completing your due diligence on the ICO's nature (see the preceding section), register for the ICO based on its website's instructions.

4. Wait for the launch date and follow the instructions. This step normally consists of transferring your cryptocurrency assets from your crypto wallet to the ICO's public address. This step may also cost a transaction fee.

5. After the ICO is launched, the team sends the new tokens to your crypto wallet.

Because of the risky nature of ICOs and the difficulty in selecting the best ones, you may consider skipping the ICO and waiting until the token/cryptocurrency is launched before buying it. Though many ICOs see an immediate and rapid surge right after launch, more often than not they come crashing down shortly after.

 The crash doesn't necessarily mean that the token isn't worthy of holding. Historically, these types of price changes happen in the tech industry quite often, providing an excellent post-launch buying opportunity. When things settle down and more people have analyzed the new token, its price can move back up slowly, giving you an opportunity to invest at your own pace. An ICO is rarely too good to pass up it (although it does happen).

Hold your tokens after your purchase

The method you choose to monitor your ICO purchase highly depends on the reasons you bought in the first place. Although not all ICOs are investment vehicles, most teams behind ICOs prefer that you don't buy and dump their tokens after the ICO, so they do whatever it takes to convince you to hold onto the tokens. And doing so may just pay off in the long run.

_____

_____

_____

If you invested in the ICO for capital gain purposes only, be prepared to hold onto your investment for a while. At first, your investment may turn negative with a loss, or it may consolidate at the same price with no real returns for a while. Often these periods of losses and consolidation are followed by a massive surge, which may give you the opportunity to take profit. Keep in mind that sometimes the big surges are the beginning of an uptrend (or more gains) in the market, so by selling too rapidly you may miss out on more profit. Other times, the surge can be a simple pump-and-dump. Therefore, you need to continuously monitor and conduct analysis to create the best exit strategy.

Note: If you make money on your ICO investment, you have to report it as capital gains. See Chapter 3 for more on taxes.

Stocks with Exposure to Cryptos

When I want to start the process of strategy development for any asset, I make sure I analyze the markets from fundamental, sentimental, and technical points of view and then add my risk tolerance and portfolio diversity to the mix to achieve a perfect, personalized strategy that works for me. The same works for picking stocks. But if you're looking specifically for stocks with exposure to the cryptocurrency/blockchain industry, you need to do the analysis on both ends — the stock itself and its crypto side. The following sections cover how you can conduct the analysis on your own.

 If you're interested in getting my up-to-date stock picks and the latest investment strategies, consider joining Invest Diva's Premium Investing Group at `https://learn.investdiva.com/join-group`.

Fundamentals

Blockchain and cryptocurrencies are related, but not all companies who are investing in blockchain technology have direct exposure to the cryptocurrency market. And even though the cryptocurrency market took a hit in 2018, major public companies continued their rapid investments in blockchain technology. In fact, when PricewaterhouseCoopers (PwC) surveyed 600 executives from 15 territories in August 2018, 84 percent of them indicated their companies were "actively involved" with blockchain technology.

As I discuss in Chapter 1, blockchain is the underlying technology for cryptocurrencies such as Bitcoin and Ethereum. In 2018, companies who were reorganizing their structure to incorporate blockchain included IBM, Accenture, Deloitte, J.P. Morgan, and HSBC, to name a few. I can only imagine more big names will have jumped on the blockchain wagon by the time you have this book in your hands. On the other hand, research from Cowen suggests blockchain won't experience widespread adoption before 2022. Therefore, doing up-to-date research when conducting fundamental analysis on this topic is crucial.

How about cryptocurrencies? How can you get indirect exposure to this byproduct of blockchain technology? You need to think outside the box. The following sections give you some points to search for before you select stocks with crypto exposure. (For more information on fundamental analysis, check out Chapter 3. You can also visit `https://learn.investdiva.com/free-webinar-3-secrets-to-making-your-money-work-for-you`.)

Companies can get involved with the cryptocurrency market in so many ways. Make sure to stay on top of the news on websites such as http://newsbtc.com to be in the know.

Crypto mining exposure

Some major cryptocurrencies are minable. And to be able to mine, you need high-end computers with sophisticated hardware, as I cover in Chapter 4. When cryptocurrency mining is at its peak, such companies' stock value also skyrockets. One example of this trend was Advanced Micro Devices stock (AMD) in 2017 and 2018. My Premium Investing Group members and I saw over 1,000 percent return over the two-year period that we held onto our AMD stocks. More specifically, we started buying AMD shares when it was $1.84 per share at the beginning of 2016 and sold throughout 2018 as it reached $25 and above. Of course, cryptocurrency mining was only one of the drivers behind AMD's price surge. But for sure, as more people got into cryptocurrency mining, the demand for AMD graphics processing units (GPUs) went higher, and so did AMD's share value.

Many other companies are now focusing on this area and may potentially do a better job than AMD in the future. Media websites such as `https://mashable.com/` often track the latest tech news, so following them can give you an edge in knowing which companies can give you crypto mining exposure.

Crypto payment exposure

Another way to get indirect exposure to the cryptocurrency market through public companies is to go after those that accept altcoins as a payment method for their services. Some pioneers in this area include Overstock.com (stock symbol: OSTK) and Microsoft (stock symbol: MSFT) in 2017 and 2018. You can find out which companies accept cryptos as payment through news sources such as Mashable (`https://mashable.com/`), NewsBTC (`http://newsbtc.com`), and MarketWatch (`www.marketwatch.com/`).

If crypto payment exposure is the *only* reason you're investing in these types of stocks, you must remember that their price volatility can be directly correlated to the cryptocurrency market itself and therefore may not give you the diversification you're looking for. For example, Overstock's OSTK shares saw massive gains after it started to accept Bitcoin at the end of 2017 and throughout the beginning of 2018. However, as the Bitcoin price crashed, so did OSTK's share price.

Crypto trading exposure

While the government authorities were trying to figure out regulations around cryptocurrencies, many public trading companies, brokers, and traditional exchanges got ahead of the crowd to offer cryptocurrency trading opportunities for the masses. For example, when Interactive Brokers Group (stock symbol: IBKR) announced on December 13, 2017, that it will allow its customers to *short* Bitcoin (sell it in speculation that its value will drop), its stock price actually dropped. The reason for that may have been that at the time, Bitcoin's price was at its peak, and most people didn't like the idea of shorting Bitcoin. Of course, Bitcoin prices ended up falling a few months later, and IBKR saw a boost in its stock price value. It then dropped again due to factors other than its Bitcoin exposure.

Speculative trading based on rumors and news can be very risky. When analyzing a stock from a fundamental point for a medium-to-long-term investment strategy, you must consider other factors, such as the company's management, services, industry outlook, financial statements, and financial ratios. I cover short-term trading strategies and long-term investing strategies earlier in this chapter.

Market sentiment factors

Market sentiment is the general behavior and "feeling" of market participants toward a specific asset such as cryptos or stocks. When searching for stocks with crypto exposure, you must measure the market sentiment not only toward that stock but also toward the cryptocurrency industry. This approach gives you an idea about the direction you can take with your investment.

For a very simplified example, say that fundamental and technical analyses are showing that you can expect the price of a given stock to go lower in the future. (The technical term for this move is a *bearish reversal* in a stock price.) But if you want to complete your analysis, you must also measure the market sentiment using shorter time frames and indicators such as Ichimoku Kinko Hyo (see www.investdiva.com/investing-guide/ichimoku-kinko-hyo-explained/ for details).

Other market sentiment indicators include the following:

- Moving average convergence divergence (MACD) (`www.investdiva.com/investing-guide/macd/`)
- Relative strength index (RSI) (`www.investdiva.com/investing-guide/relative-strength-index-rsi/`)
- Bollinger Bands (BOL) (`www.investdiva.com/investing-guide/bollinger-bands-bol/`)

Other considerations

At the end of the day, if you're looking to create a well-diversified portfolio by getting indirect exposure to cryptocurrencies, you may want to avoid *double dipping* (investing in the same category/industry twice). Stocks with exposure to cryptos should only be a proportionate piece of your overall portfolio, as categorized by industry. If you're looking to get an idea of how much you'll make on your investment with the amount of risk you're taking, and how much you should value the company's stock price, you must analyze the industry properly. Then you can focus on picking the best stock in that category.

Here are some questions to ask before picking the top crypto related stocks for your portfolio:

- Is the company working on any new developments in its technology?
- What impact are potential breakthroughs likely to have?
- Is the demand for the crypto related services related to key economic variables? If so, which ones?
- How much is the company planning to spend on crypto related services? How is it planning to fund that spending?
- Is the company rapidly employing and opening new crypto/blockchain-related jobs?

You can find the answers to these questions by researching the company's press releases and public reports. Your broker may also help you get your hands on the most recent developments. Of course, at Invest Diva, I also try to stay on top of all the developments, so make sure you subscribe to my free updates at `https://learn.investdiva.com/start`.

_____

_____

_____

Cryptocurrency and Blockchain ETFs

If you're having a hard time picking the right stock, then you may want to consider another option. One of the easiest ways to get exposure to a specific industry without having to pick the top assets in that category is trading an exchange traded fund, or ETF. An ETF is similar to a mutual fund in that they're both "baskets" of assets in the same category. But ETFs are becoming more popular for reasons such as the following:

- They're more tax efficient than mutual funds.
- They have lower trading expenses compared to those of mutual funds.
- They're simpler/more flexible than mutual funds.
- They're more accessible than mutual funds to an average investor.

In the following sections, I introduce you to ETFs and other indexes that provide exposure to cryptocurrencies and blockchain technology.

An overview of blockchain ETFs

In 2018, a handful of blockchain-related ETFs were accessible to individual investors. However, Bitcoin ETFs or cryptocurrency ETFs didn't have much luck getting regulated, even though many of them were in line to get approval from the Securities and Exchange Commission (SEC). That's why investors who really wanted exposure to the crypto industry through an ETF had to look for the next best thing, which was a blockchain ETF.

The first blockchain ETFs to hit the markets were BLOK and BLCN, both of which launched on January 17, 2018 (right at the time when Bitcoin was taking a hit). On January 29, 2018, another blockchain ETF, KOIN, showed its face in the competition. Here's a brief introduction to these three ETFs:

- BLOK's full name is the Amplify Transformational Data Shearing ETF. Its basket holds 52 assets, including Digital Garage, Inc. (stock symbol: DLGEF), GMO Internet, Inc. (stock symbol: GMOYF), and Square, Inc. (stock symbol: SQ). You can find the most recent updates to this ETF at www.marketwatch.com/investing/fund/blok.

- BLCN's full name is the Reality Shares Nasdaq NexGen Economy ETF. Its top holdings have more attractive stocks with blockchain exposure, including Advanced Micro Devices, Inc. (stock symbol: AMD), Intel Corporation (stock symbol: INTC), Microsoft Corporation (stock symbol: MSFT), and SBI Holdings, Inc. (stock symbol: SBHGF). You can find the most recent developments in this ETF at `https://finance.yahoo.com/quote/BLCN/holdings/`.

- KOIN's full name is Innovation Shares NextGen Protocol ETF. This one didn't get as much love as the other two ETFs at the beginning. Its top holdings include Taiwan Semiconductor Manufacturing Co. Ltd. ADR (stock symbol: TSM), Amazon (stock symbol: AMZN), Nvidia (stock symbol: NVDA), Microsoft, and Cisco Systems (stock symbol: CSCO).

  This option, to me, looks like a pretty good selection because of its focus on artificial intelligence. But perhaps the reason investors weren't as lovey-dovey with this ETF at the beginning was that it appears to have the least amount of direct exposure to the blockchain industry when compared to the other two.

However, its returns surpassed that of BLOK and BLCN by September 2018. You can find out about the most recent developments in KOIN at `www.morningstar.com/etfs/ARCX/KOIN/quote.html`.

Disclaimer: I personally own AMD, INTC, NVDA, AMZN, and MSFT in my portfolio as of 2018.

These three ETFs had the early-arrival advantage for some time, but that doesn't necessarily mean they're the best in the game.

Investing in ETFs makes the stock-analysis process a bit easier, but you still need a general understanding of ETFs' holding companies in order to be able to pick the one that best suits your portfolio. If various ETFs' holdings are widely different even in the same industry, you may want to consider investing in multiple ETFs, as long as their prices aren't correlated.

Other indexes

While cryptocurrency ETFs take their time to get regulatory approval, you can look for other indexes in the industry that can give you exposure to the crypto market. For example, in March 2018, Coinbase — one

of the largest crypto exchanges in the United States —
announced that it was planning to launch its own
index fund. The index aimed to follow all the digital
assets listed on Coinbase's exchange, GDAX, which
at the time included Bitcoin, Litecoin, Ethereum, and
Bitcoin Cash. However, in October 2018 the exchange
had to shut down the index due to lack of industrial
interest. Instead, it's shifting its focus to a new retail
product. Stay ahead of these types of announcements
by subscribing to my mailing list (`https://learn.`
`investdiva.com/start`). Here are some other
cryptocurrency news sources in alphabetical order:

- `https://www.cnbc.com/`
- `https://www.coindesk.com/`
- `https://www.forbes.com/`
  `crypto-blockchain/`
- `https://www.investing.com/news/`
  `cryptocurrency-news`
- `https://www.nasdaq.com/topic/`
  `cryptocurrency`
- `https://www.newsbtc.com/`

About the Author

Kiana Danial is an award-winning, internationally recognized personal investing and wealth management expert. She is a highly sought-after professional speaker, author, and executive coach who delivers workshops and seminars to corporations, universities, and entrepreneurial groups. She is a frequent expert on many TV and radio stations and has reported on the financial markets directly from the floor of the New York Stock Exchange and Nasdaq. She has a daily cryptocurrency online video show on the London-based cryptocurrency media portal NewsBTC and is a weekly investment expert guest on Tokyo's number one investment TV show. Her cryptocurrency strategies are featured on Nasdaq.com, Investing.com, and FXStreet.com, among others, on a daily basis. She has been featured in *The Wall Street Journal*, *Time*, CNN, *Forbes*, *TheStreet*, and numerous other publications and media outlets.

Dedication

To my sister, Ana, and to Mother,
whose loss I so keenly felt yet at times
denied. Thank you for making
me connect again.

"

**RATIONAL THOUGHTS
NEVER DRIVE PEOPLE'S
CREATIVITY THE WAY**

EMOTIONS DO

NEIL DEGRASSE TYSON
ASTROPHYSICIST

connecting
/kuh-nekting/

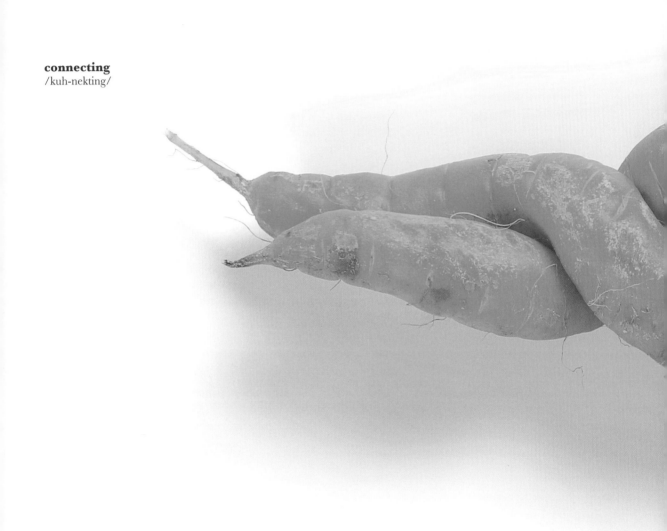

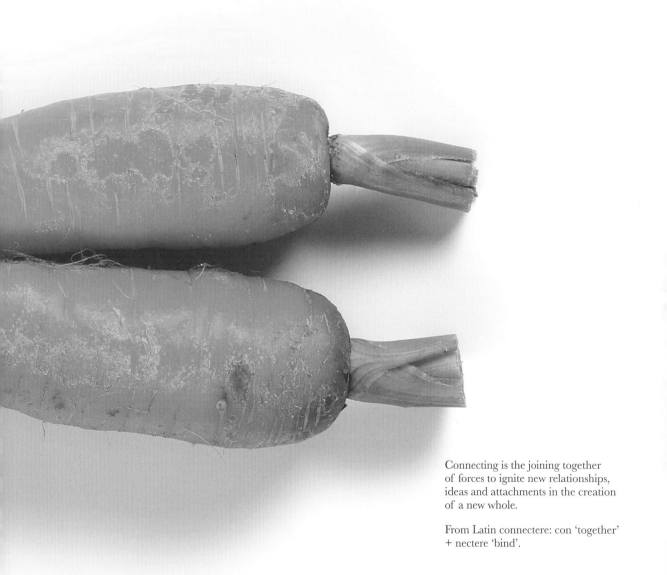

Connecting is the joining together
of forces to ignite new relationships,
ideas and attachments in the creation
of a new whole.

From Latin connectere: con 'together'
+ nectere 'bind'.

THE GOOD, BAD AND UGLY

Connecting explores the paradoxical nature of our creativity – so we ask you, the reader, to release your expectations.

Parts of *Connecting* are personal and others are metaphorical and practical. Our hope is it will confound, confuse and uplift you – but most of all that it awakens you to the full range of your emotions so you can connect with your creative powers.

CONNECTING IS AN HOMAGE TO OUR CREATIVE FORCES. EACH PAGE IS A DELECTABLE MORSEL DESIGNED TO ENLIGHTEN, ILLUMINATE, CHALLENGE AND PROVOKE.

YOU CAN START ANYWHERE, DIP IN AND OUT OR READ IT END TO END.

LET YOUR INTUITION BE YOUR GUIDE.

CONTENTS

FOREWORD

Connecting is an anti-road map to creative cultivation, full of mind-expanding paradoxes and soul-stimulating symbols that beautifully fail to answer any of our questions and instead pose much greater ones, creating a space for true creative explosiveness. It is a riotous immersion in the power of emotions to propel our creativity.

Paulina Larocca is a rare creative creature with a sorceress-like ability to unlock our truths, ourselves and our universal creative potential.

James Kerley
Creative Director, Author,
Storyteller and Executive Producer

THE PARADOXICAL NATURE OF OUR CREATIVITY

ONE

"THERE CAN BE NO KNOWLEDGE WITHOUT EMOTION. :)

WE MAY BE AWARE
OF A TRUTH, YET
UNTIL WE HAVE
FELT ITS FORCE, IT
IS NOT OURS. TO
THE COGNITION OF
THE BRAIN MUST
BE ADDED THE
EXPERIENCE OF
THE SOUL."
+

ARNOLD BENNETT
NOVELIST

**CREATIVITY AIN'T
NO JOYRIDE**

We crave connections. We are, arguably, the most socially connected generation in history, yet mental health afflictions are on the rise. Why?

In part, because our emotional palette is increasingly stunted. We have a fixation with happiness but our creativity needs to feast on all of our emotions to thrive.

We think happiness is what we want, when what we deeply desire is to feel more alive.

CREATIVITY IS A MIXED BAG

Groundbreaking studies by psychologists and neuroscientists are unravelling the mysteries of the creative mind and the results are confounding. It appears the longstanding view that positive emotions are conducive to fostering creativity is maddeningly incomplete.

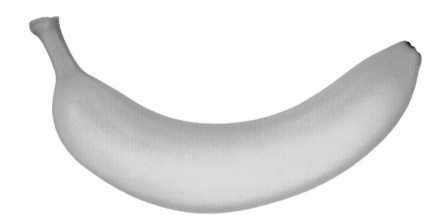

While being creative might make us feel good, to be more creative we also need to feel bad. Frustration, anger and sorrow are all fuel for the creative mill and when they are combined with their opposites – equanimity, love and joy – that is when our creativity explodes.

CREATIVITY IS PARADOXICAL

Science is finding that highly creative people, as measured by creative achievement, are paradoxical thinkers. When engaged in creative acts, they are diverging (exploring new ideas) and converging (selecting promising possibilities) simultaneously.

As the late American author F. Scott Fitzgerald said, "The test of a first-rate intelligence is the ability to hold two opposed ideas in mind at the same time and still retain the ability to function."

TWO-FACED

Science has discovered that creative people are also more in touch with their emotions. Not only do they feel them with greater intensity, they often experience conflicting emotions – for example, joy and sorrow – at the same time.

This paradoxical way of being calls to mind Janus, the two-faced Roman god of beginnings and endings, who was able to embody all possibilities – the past and the future – at once.

When we are confronted with contradictions or paradoxes, most of us struggle to maintain a sense of unity, but these fissures nourish creative inspiration, forcing us to accept new realities in order to resolve the oppositions.

CREATIVITY
IS DYING TO
GET OUT

Creativity and our emotional health are linked. The more we reduce our emotional range, the more we constrict our creativity – which relies on our ability to feel all of our emotions.

Not surprisingly, mental health afflictions are on the rise, with depression now the leading cause of disability worldwide.

To be creative, you must be emotionally alive. That means embracing all of your feelings – even the dark, uncomfortable ones that make you feel dead inside – because within them also resides the light.

FEEL

WITHOUT THINKING

ING

It seems the more we learn about creativity, the more it continues to confound and defy. To embrace our creative powers fully, we have to accept that it is not enough to think.

Instead, we need to embody the full spectrum of our emotions, from the riotous and intense ones that make us feel cut adrift in a raging storm to the soft and mournful feelings that like to creep alongside us, waiting for their moment to pounce when we are least aware.

DON'T LEAVE ME HANGING

It might seem scary at first, but you need to expose yourself creatively.

Don't be afraid to ask for feedback. Even though it can be painful (especially if it is something that is personal and meaningful), embracing it can propel you to new heights.

Let go of your misconceptions of what the feedback should be and set aside your assumptions. Allow your creation to take its own path and find its own destiny. Feedback is all part of the creative process of learning and discovery.

HURTS
SO GOOD

Our emotions have the ability to become a personal symphony, where each feeling has its part but they collectively become a transcendent orchestra that reverberates within us to create new meaning.

To dare to embody our emotions this fully is a creative person's path. It is tempestuous and rocky but the price of not feeling this deeply is an even greater cost to bear.

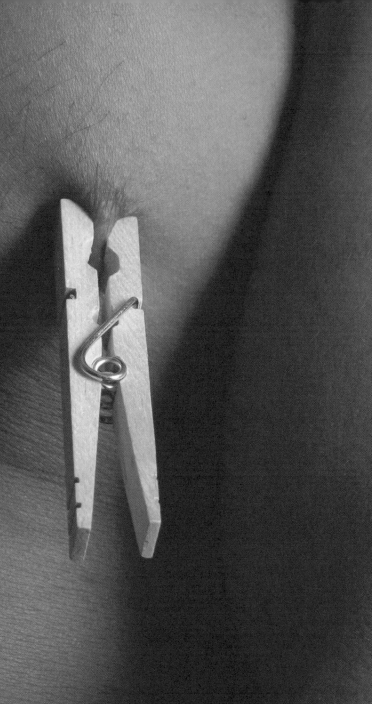

HANIF KUREISHI
NOVELIST

"IT'S FRUSTRAT WHICH MAKES CREATIVI POSSIBLE

CREATIVE HELL

TWO

39

"AFTER ALL THESE YEARS, I HAVE COME TO REALISE THAT I MUST GO THROUGH A PERIOD OF AGONY AND **TORTURE** BEFORE I HAVE A BREAKTHROUGH."

HANS ZIMMER
COMPOSER

DEATH

IS A POWERFUL CATALYST FOR CREATIVITY

This book was conceived five years ago, when my sister was in the final stages of dying from the motor neuron disease amyotrophic lateral sclerosis (ALS).

It is so unfair. You struggle to comprehend it. In some ways, you have no choice but to laugh at times, otherwise all you would do is cry. So you laugh, cry, live and die all at the same time – and isn't that what the creative process is all about? Facing death gives you an incredible hunger for life.

GRIEF AND CREATIVITY ARE STRANGE BEDFELLOWS

As profoundly tragic as it was to lose my sister, it was also surprisingly cathartic. In our society, grief is a private affair and we are expected to keep a lid on our emotions. But hiding from death makes it seem threatening and horrific.

In other cultures, grief is accompanied by an outpouring of emotion – even celebrations. As strange as it might seem, being able to express the powerful and conflicting feelings in an open and unrestrained way provides the necessary catharsis for the relief of the pain. Grief and creativity are deeply intertwined.

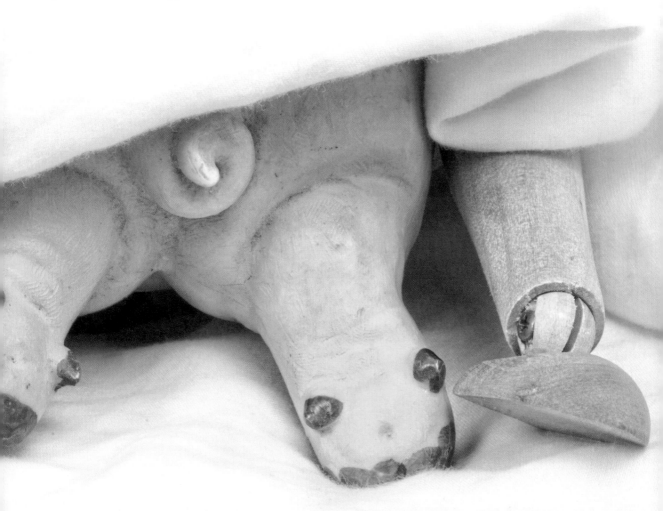

Grief is a creative rush because it releases an emotional symphony of conflicted feelings – from sorrow, hopelessness, loneliness, vulnerability and rawness to renewal, release, reverence, reconciliation and joyousness.

It is, at once, tragic, poignant, humorous and nonsensical.

PAIR

47

Five years after my sister died, I finally worked up the courage to start to write *Connecting*. The creative process was not straightforward. At first, it flowed, but then, inexplicably, it came to a halt. It seemed my creativity had dried up.

Then, unexpectedly, my mother suffered a severe stroke and died. Oh, the sweet, tragic irony! I was once again facing monumental loss and being forced to confront – and connect with – my emotions.

CREATIVITY IS NO LAUGHING MATTER

Living without creativity

would be a living hell.

Facing death again got my creative
juices flowing again. First a drop,
then a trickle, then a torrent.

I could only conclude that tragedy is
the universe's way of showing off
its creative flair.

**DYING
TO FEEL**

"THE BEST AND MOST BEAUTIFUL THINGS IN THE WORLD CANNOT BE SEEN OR EVEN TOUCHED.

THEY MUST BE FELT WITH THE HEART."

HELEN KELLER
AUTHOR

UNLEASHING OUR CREATIVITY

THREE

"THERE IS NO PERFECTION, ONLY BEAUTIFUL VERSIONS OF BROKENNESS."

SHANNON L. ALDER
AUTHOR

58

59

BURN

ING

DOWN THE HOUSE

Creativity is Prometheus' fire – a force so powerful that it could only be entrusted to the gods. It is knowing, it is being; wielding it is to give breath to life itself – the greatest rebellion in existence. To express it takes fearlessness but to deny it is to deaden the emotional richness of our lives.

The ability to capture and convey the emotional landscape of our innermost thoughts is what sets us, humans, apart. Our mind's interconnected web of perceptions, beliefs and emotions fuels our creativity. Its transformative power shapes us as individuals and can alter the course of civilisation.

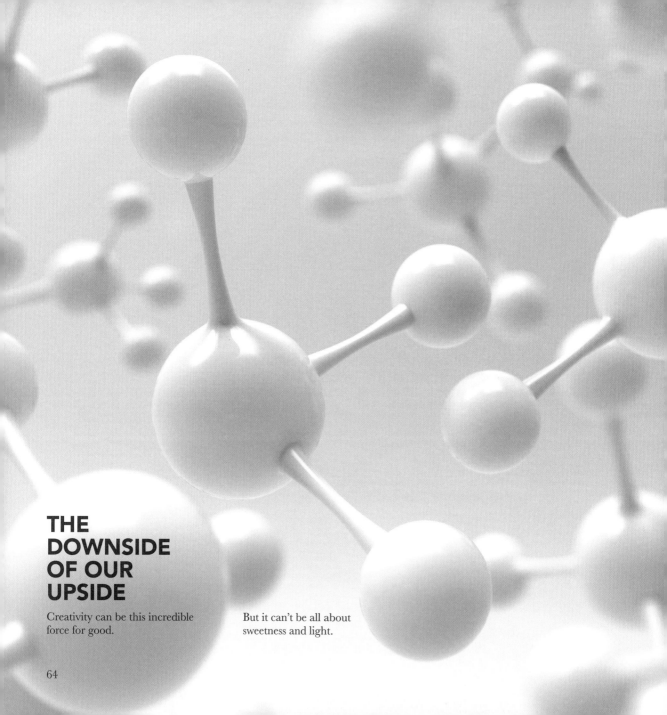

THE
DOWNSIDE
OF OUR
UPSIDE

Creativity can be this incredible
force for good.

But it can't be all about
sweetness and light.

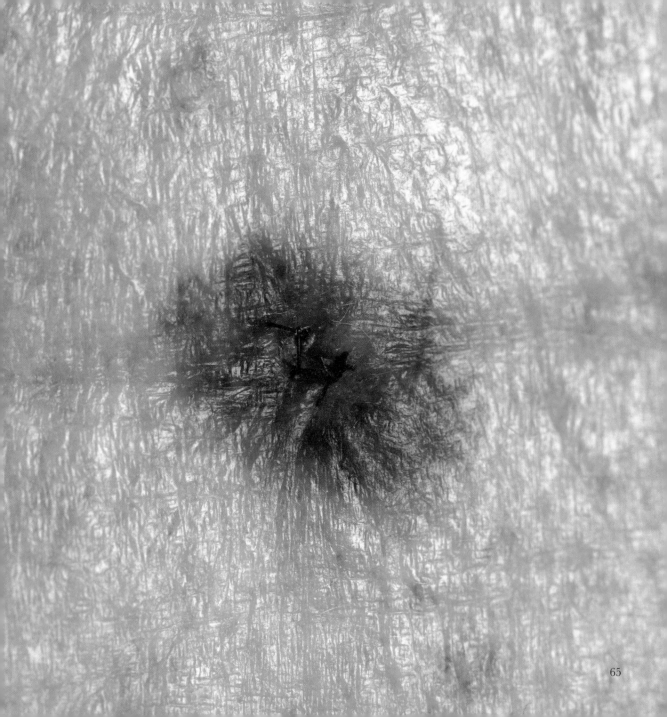

65

HEAVEN

THE BEAUTY OF CONTRADICTIONS

HELL

For our civilisation to survive, we must engage more deeply with our creative nature. We must accept that both demon and god reside in each one of us and our emotional landscape traverses both heaven and hell. Until we can hold up a mirror to our true nature, the canvas of our creativity will not reveal itself. When we can see our virtues and vices reflected back to us, creativity will make its second coming.

We are taught how to think but not how to feel. Instead, we are taught what to feel and that the darker emotions, like anger, frustration, fear and sadness are less socially acceptable than the lighter emotions of joy, happiness and surprise.

CREATIVITY FEASTS ON OUR

EMOT

IONS

OUR
CREATIVITY
IS STARVING

Our diet of political correctness –
when it comes to emotions – is dulling
our creativity. We put ourselves on
a restrictive emotional diet and then
wonder why we are constantly hungry
and craving something more.

71

LIBER

Creativity is a life-giving force that frees us from our conditioned thinking. We tend to think about creativity as conceiving and creating new ideas, but it is much more than that.

Creativity is an energetic state that vibrates inside our body, influencing our mood. It is never static. Contained within this vibration are all of the emotions of life, not just the 'feel good' ones.

ATING

THE CHANGING FACE OF OUR CREATIVE NATURE

Emotions are not inherently good or bad. They are all necessary for our survival. If we didn't have anger, we could not defend ourselves – nor could we understand its opposite, which is love and acceptance.

Because we now view emotions through the lens of political correctness, we are developing cultural antibodies to the passionate, hedonistic sensations of our existence. Living with intense feeling not only nourishes creativity, it helps give rise to our greatest cultural accomplishments.

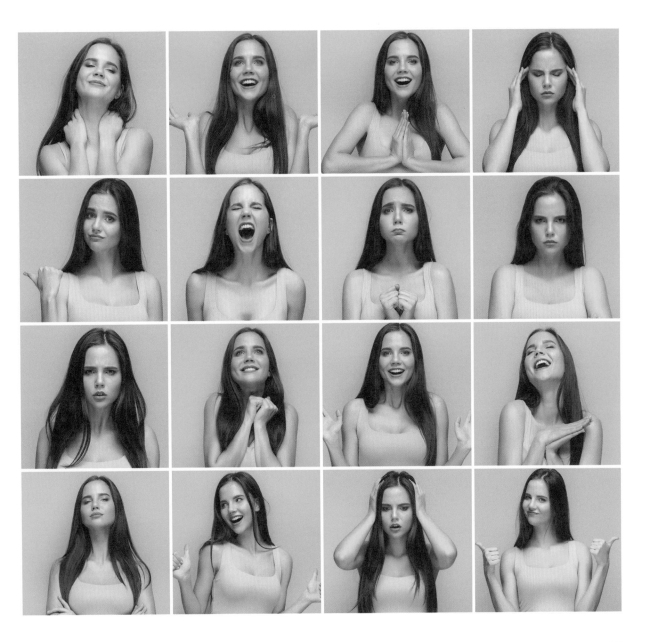

Many of us struggle to identify what exactly we are feeling. There are a variety of reasons why this is so difficult. We've been trained to believe that strong emotions should be suppressed. We have certain (sometimes unspoken) societal and organisational rules against expressing them. Or we've never learned a language (visual, verbal, kinaesthetic) to describe our emotions accurately.

This inability to express our emotions fully also has an impact on our creativity; the ability to feel a range of emotions intensely is a distinguishing trait of highly creative individuals.

WE'VE BEEN TRAINED TO BELIEVE THAT STRONG EMOTIONS SHOULD BE...

SUPPRESSED

TECHNOLOGY CANNOT

CONQUER

ALL

The greatest achievement of modern man is the ability to control, alter and bend our environment to our will. Seemingly nothing is unconquerable – from the outer reaches of the universe to the subatomic world. It's all thanks to our creative powers in service to science and technology.

Despite these extraordinary powers, however, it feels our daily lives are veering out of control. We are overwhelmed by the changes technology has ignited. It was supposed to put us in the driver's seat. Instead, it is driving us at a pace we find punishingly hard to endure.

79

CREATIVITY
CONTAINS THE
MYSTERIES
OF THE

UNIVERSE

CREATIVITY IS THE AWAKENING OF OUR CONSCIOUSNESS TO THE *MYSTERIUM TREMENDUM ET FASCINANS* – THE KNOWING THAT WE CANNOT RATIONALISE, WHICH IS TERRIFYINGLY POWERFUL, BUT ALSO MERCIFUL AND GRACIOUS IN ITS GIFTS.

If our gadgets cannot keep us from feeling bad, we have a cocktail of other choices to alter our mood, including drugs such as opioids, amphetamines and cannabis – to name a few. We also have temptations to overindulge in, such as sugar, alcohol, fat and caffeine. They all have unwelcome side effects, but we continue to consume them because we are desperate to reset our emotional thermostat.

ANYTHING TO STOP FEELING

Yet the more we stop feeling, the more we cut ourselves off from our life-giving force – creativity.

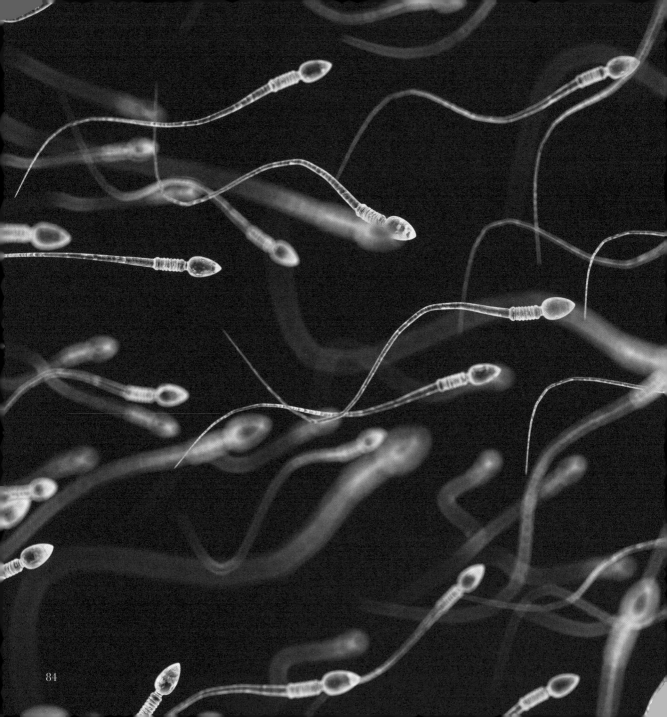

RELEASE OUR CREATIVE CONSTRAINTS

Creativity and our emotional health are linked. The more we increase our emotional range, the more suffering we can endure and the more we release our creativity — which relies on our ability to feel all of our emotions intensely.

KILL YOUR DOUBTS
BEFORE THEY KILL YOU

When you embark on a creative project, you will experience that nagging 'you are not good enough' feeling, because you will never achieve the level of perfection you see in your mind. This type of thinking can be deadly, because it prevents you from trying and failing. Both are required for creativity.

Your feelings of inadequacy are a gift because when harnessed properly, they propel you to act. Inertia, not fear, is the enemy of creation.

The myth of the

MUSE

The Greeks created the Muses to ease the suffering of mankind by mesmerising them with nymph-like creatures that embodied the artistic ideals of grace and beauty.

They have come to represent what we want creative inspiration to be like, preventing us from accepting that the most beautiful things are often born from that which is disturbing, uncomfortable, disagreeable and discordant.

Only when we embrace this knowledge can the full promise of our creative potential be realised.

WITHOUT UGLINESS THERE CAN BE NO BEAUTY

We don't want to know our dark, deformed and detestable side. But every act of creation forces us to concede that what sets us apart is the suffering we have endured and have caused. It's an uncomfortable truth that is rarely acknowledged.

The products of our creativity might be lyrical and sublime, but that can be a far cry from the energy that birthed them.

91

CREATIVITY'S BATTLE WITH TECHNOLOGY

To ease our pain, we create more innovations to buffer us from our environment, locking us in a vicious cycle with technology. We are addicted to its ability to increase our comforts and provide quick fixes, which is making us more short-tempered and impatient. Studies have shown the more comfortable our life is, the less we can cope with "problems" like traffic or slow internet.

WE ARE DAMAGED AND OUR CREATIVITY IS SUFFERING

Our mental health is suffering. Depression has reached epidemic proportions; 300 million people are suffering with it, making it the leading cause of disability, globally.

Physically, we are living longer, but we get sicker at an earlier age, due to the increasing prevalence of lifestyle diseases, caused by preventable illnesses, such as obesity, that affect our quality of life.

Without healthy bodies or minds, it is no wonder our creativity is suffering.

ESCAPING THE EMOTIONAL LOWS LIMITS OUR CREATIVITY

A life free of passions is a life not worth living. If you want to be happier, more expressive and free, you need to have experienced profound sorrow, loss and grief. When you try to escape the emotional lows of life, you limit the highs and unwittingly curtail your creativity.

STI
FLI
NG

CREATIVITY

Technology is stifling creativity. Western civilisation is at a crossroads. We have enshrined freedom of expression, yet many of us feel cut off, disconnected and unable to coherently construct a life with meaning. It is hard to be creative when our emotions are cauterised.

We are using our knowledge to create and support technology to distance ourselves from each other, our feelings and the dark musings of our private nature. So much of our creative energy is now bound up in presenting ourselves to the world through a sanitised lens that lacks any semblance of cogent truth.

The act of creation can be soul destroying.

All your fears, doubts and insecurities become demons who claw, rip and tear at your fragile mask, seeking to expose you.

'You have nothing to offer.'

'You are useless.'

'You're a fraud.'

These hideous words reverberate in your head, causing your stomach to revolt.

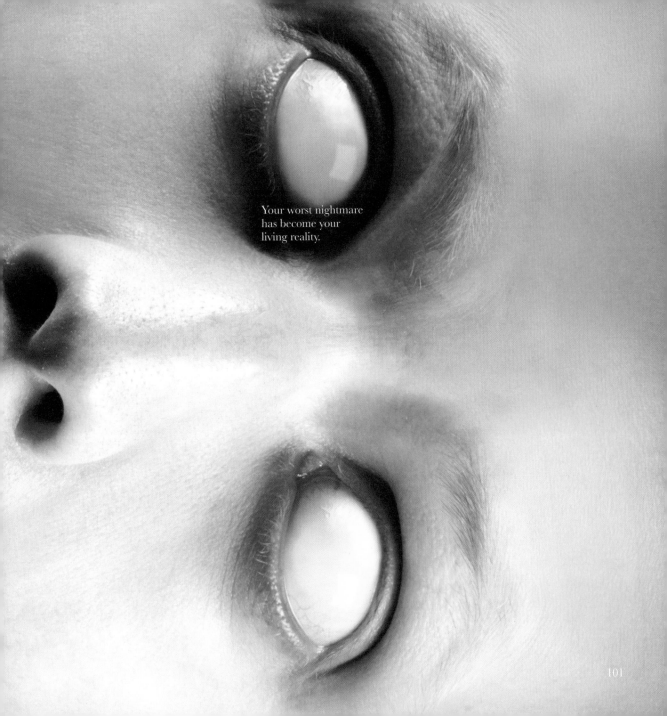

Your worst nightmare
has become your
living reality.

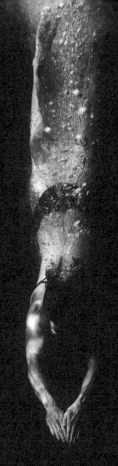

The creative act is often associated with the birth of the new idea; however, it is the act of conception – that fuzzy moment when your perception shifts – when the real change happens. The knowledge gained cannot be undone. Our world is forever changed when our body and brain are permanently altered by the shift in our mind. Is it any wonder that we have a quasi-religious relationship with creativity?

SEEING BENEATH THE SURFACE

"EVERY ACT OF CREATION IS FIRST OF ALL AN ACT OF DESTRUCTION!

CONNECTING THE DOTS

FOUR

"MANY IDEAS GROW BETTER WHEN

TRANSPLANTED INTO ANOTHER MIND THAN IN THE ONE WHERE THEY SPRANG UP."

OLIVER WENDELL HOLMES, SR.
AUTHOR

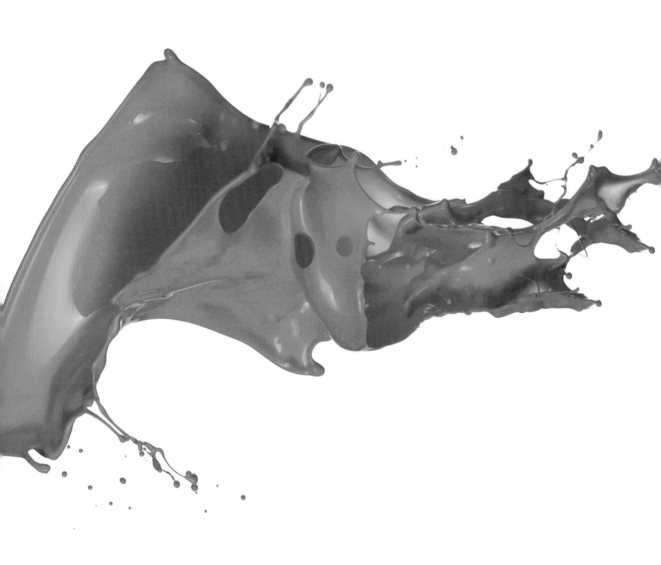

STOP THE SABOTAGE

Creative blocks bring up all kinds of feelings of inadequacy – dark, negative thoughts.

As tempting as it is, the one thing you cannot do is quit, regardless of how much you think you suck at this. Otherwise, your creativity will die a premature death.

SACRIFICE

SAF

ETY

**TO RELEASE
CREATIVITY**

THINK
LESS

When your brain is distracted by your body, your creative thoughts will well up.

Get your creative process rolling by going for a walk or run, take a nap, fidget, jump up and down, scream, laugh, rip your hair out, roar…

**FEEL
MORE**

UNLEASH

CULTURAL CONSTRAINTS

Creativity flourishes when the prevailing cultural canon is one of questioning and experimentation, as this imbues life with meaning. We must be careful not to accept cultural constraints, which can impose a rigid orthodoxy that coerces, corrals and corrects us, stunting our creative growth.

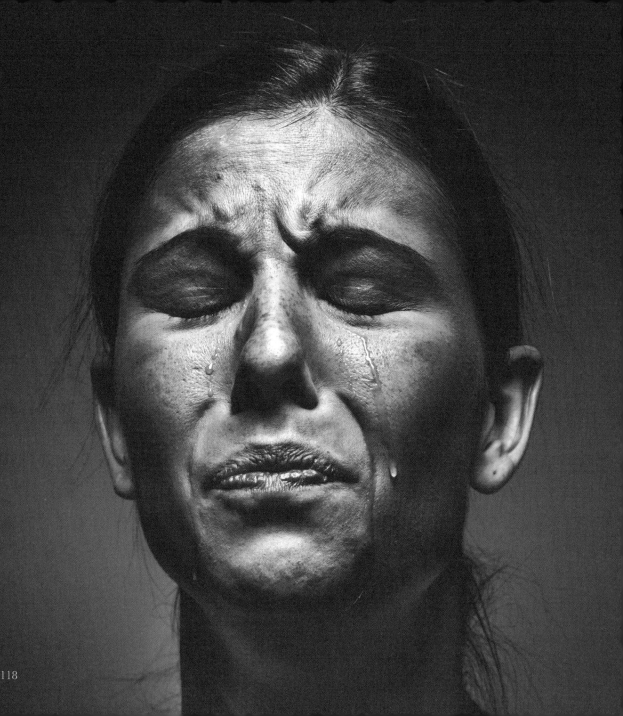

DON'T SUFFER

IN SILENCE

Our creative genius is our ability to make our emotions the centrepiece of our personal narrative and give meaning and life to what would otherwise be too oppressive to bear. It is our sorrows that shape us and make our joys stupendous in contrast. And it is our creativity that provides the resilience to enable us to embody it all.

ACCEPT THAT CREATIVITY WON'T COME ON COMMAND

Creativity has a dark side. It cannot be mastered with wilfulness. It does not come on demand or by command. Creativity springs the lock only when we accept that we are not its master.

Give birth to lots of ideas and don't be afraid to share them. It might seem scary at first, but you need to expose yourself creatively. Embrace feedback even though it can be painful, as it can propel your creativity to new heights. The more ideas you spawn, the less afraid you'll be to let them…

LIVE

OR
DIE

123

Seek out emotional intensity, as it
feeds our creativity. Highs of toe-
curling intensity can be realised only
by also experiencing the inevitable
spasms of heart-numbing grief.
Contained in our emotional storms
is our capacity for creativity.

FEELING IS
FOREPLAY

IN CREATIVITY WE TRUST

We must make a conscious choice to nurture it. Ensure that we allocate time for traversing our inner world and develop a creative practice without the expectation it must lead to something.

The practice itself is a creative act. We need to do it for our mental health, for our sanity and for our society.

THE COURAGE

TO CREATE

CREATIVITY'S FLAME
IS FLICKERING

The more we neglect our emotional life, the more we dampen the creative fire that fuels and enriches life beyond all measure.

After every creative insight comes a period of readjustment when we integrate, orient and anchor ourselves in the world again. However, a creative life is a restless one. It won't be long before the world becomes too small again and we find ourselves bumping up against the walls, desperately searching for ways out. We may not always like what is on the outside – but living small is not an option. Whether we like it or not, we must press on.

A

CREATIVE

LIFE

IS

RESTLESS

133

"WE DON'T SEE THINGS AS THEY ARE,

WE SEE THEM AS WE ARE."

*ANAÏS NIN
AUTHOR*

SEVEN CREATIVE PARADOXES

FIVE

"BE COMFORTA
AND EMBRAC
CONTRADICTI
AMBIGUITY. IT
OF CREATIVIT

...BLE WITH
...PARADOX,
...ON, AND
...IS THE WOMB

DEEPAK CHOPRA
AUTHOR

139

INTRODUCTION

Like our emotions, creativity is paradoxical. A recent neuroscience study led by Roger Beaty suggests that creative people have greater connections between two areas of the brain that are typically at odds: the brain network of regions associated with focus and attentional control and the brain network of regions associated with imagination and spontaneity.

Creative people aren't characterised
by any one of these states alone; they
are characterised by their ability to mix
seemingly incompatible states. In this
section, we explore seven paradoxical
emotional states to invite you to have a
visceral experience with your creativity.

PARADOXES
SUPERCHARGE
THE BRAIN

PARADOXES ARE SO CONFOUNDING THAT THE ONLY WAY WE CAN RESOLVE THEM IS BY HARNESSING OUR CREATIVITY, WHICH ENABLES US TO REFRAME OUR REALITY TO EMBRACE THE OPPOSITION.

PARADOXES, AS PSYCHOLOGISTS HAVE FOUND, ARE ATTRACTIVE TO THE HUMAN MIND BECAUSE THEY CHALLENGE EXPECTATIONS. WHEN THE BRAIN ENCOUNTERS CONTRADICTIONS, OUR EMOTIONS JUMP OUT OF THEIR BOX.

CREATIVITY IS THE ABILITY
TO HOLD TWO OPPOSING
IDEAS IN THE MIND AT
THE SAME TIME AND
STILL RETAIN THE ABILITY
TO FUNCTION.

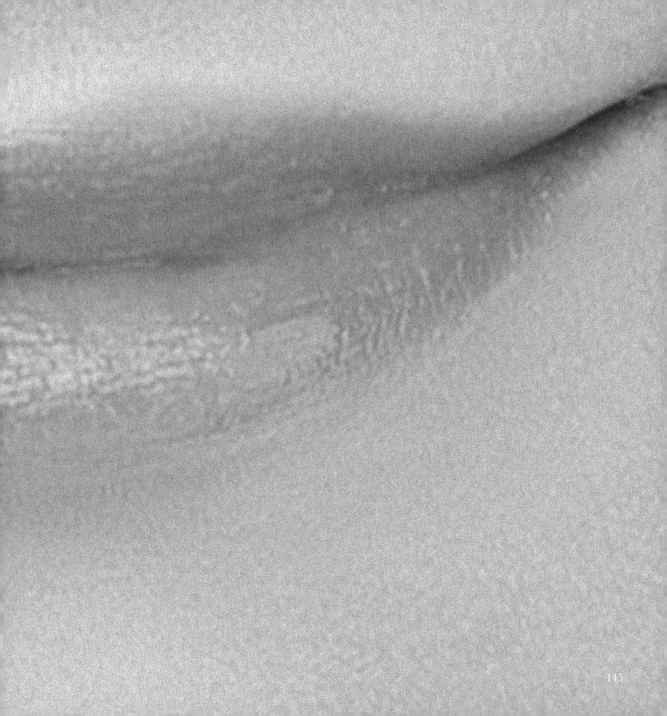

7 CREATIVE PARADOXES

RIGID AND FLEXIBLE
HUMOUR AND DESPAIR
MINDFULNESS AND DAYDREAMING
INTENSE REBELLIOUSNESS AND TRADITION
PASSION AND DISCERNMENT
INTUITION AND RATIONALITY
OPEN ATTENTION AND FOCUSED DRIVE

RIGID

AND FLEXIBLE

HUMOUR
AND
DESPAIR

MINDFULNESS

AND
DAYDREAMING

REBELLIO

USNESS

PASSION AND
DISCERNMENT

INTUITION AND RATIONALITY

OPEN ATTENTION

& FOCUSED DRIVE ●

THE END

Paulina Larocca is a leading creativity consultant and trainer with more than 15 years' experience delivering innovation for multi-national corporations. She is also a sought-after speaker on creating a more innovative culture. She has a Master of Science in Creativity and Change Leadership from Buffalo State University and is a graduate of THNK Creative Leadership School in Amsterdam, which focuses on creative leadership as applied to social change. She consults to organisations and works as an executive coach. She is also the author of *Creativity+ Catalyst for Creative Thinking*.

Paulina lives in Sydney, Australia, but works all over the world.

For more information:
www.paulinalarocca.com

Tony Ibbotson is Creative Director and the founder of The Creative Method design agency established in 2005 and is now recognised as one of Sydney's best design agencies.

The agency focuses on creating intelligently disruptive work in the new product development space for some of the world's largest consumer brands. Tony's philosophy is to tell stories and create emotional connections through big ideas and the best possible execution.

Tony has won a number of awards both nationally and internationally and has featured in a mountain of publications globally.

Tony is a New Zealander, but lives in Sydney, Australia.

For more information:
www.thecreativemethod.com

Acknowledgement to Kristina Dryza for her creative input.

BIS Publishers

Building Het Sieraad
Postjesweg 1
1057 DT Amsterdam
The Netherlands
T +31 (0)20 515 02 30
bis@bispublishers.com
www.bispublishers.com

BISPUBLISHERS

ISBN 978 90 6369 526 2